500 ENAMELED OBJECTS

500 ENAMELED OBJECTS

A CELEBRATION OF COLOR ON METAL

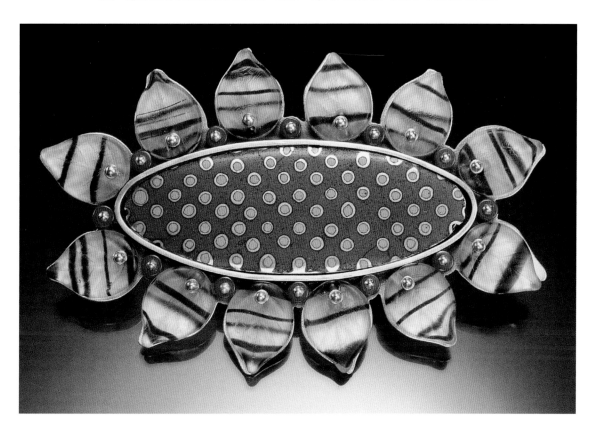

LARK
BOOKS

A Division of Sterling Publishing Co., Inc.
New York / London

SENIOR EDITOR
Marthe Le Van

EDITOR
Julie Hale

ART DIRECTOR
Matt Shay

COVER DESIGNER
Matt Shay

FRONT COVER
Jessica Calderwood *Flowers* (Platter), 2007

SPINE
Carolyn Currin Untitled Brooch, 2007

BACK COVER, TOP
Linda Darty *Outside In: Branches*, 2007

BACK COVER, BOTTOM LEFT
Catherine Elizabeth Galloway *Tile Earrings*, 2007

BACK COVER, BOTTOM CENTER
Angela Gerhard *Fozzy Bracelets*, 2007

BACK COVER, BOTTOM RIGHT
Miel-Margarita Paredes *Deliberate*, 2004

FRONT FLAP, TOP
Angela Gerhard *Red Flower Brooch*, 2008

FRONT FLAP, BOTTOM
Harlan W. Butt *Earth Beneath Our Feet: Maine Teapot #1*, 2007

BACK FLAP, TOP
Michael Romanik *White-Breasted Nuthatch* (Brooch), 2006

BACK FLAP, BOTTOM
Gretchen Goss *Gesture + Ornament: Fagus sylvatica/Pyrus alnifolia*, 2006

TITLE PAGE
Barbara Minor *Zinnia—Pin/Pendant*, 2007

OPPOSITE
Susie Ganch *Reach*, 2007

Library of Congress Cataloging-in-Publication Data

500 enameled objects : a celebration of color on metal.
    p. cm.
  "Senior editor, Marthe Le Van" --T.p. verso.
  ISBN 978-1-60059-345-1 (pb-pbk. with flaps : alk. paper)
  1. Enamel and enameling--Catalogs. I. Le Van, Marthe. II. Title: Five hundred enameled objects.
  NK5000.A15 2009
  666'.2--dc22
                                        2008031976

10 9 8 7 6 5 4 3 2 1

First Edition

Published by Lark Books, A Division of
Sterling Publishing Co., Inc.
387 Park Avenue South, New York, NY 10016

Text © 2009, Lark Books
Photography © 2009, Artist/Photographer

Distributed in Canada by Sterling Publishing,
c/o Canadian Manda Group, 165 Dufferin Street
Toronto, Ontario, Canada M6K 3H6

Distributed in the United Kingdom by GMC Distribution Services,
Castle Place, 166 High Street, Lewes, East Sussex, England BN7 1XU

Distributed in Australia by Capricorn Link (Australia) Pty Ltd.,
P.O. Box 704, Windsor, NSW 2756 Australia

If you have questions or comments about this book, please contact:
Lark Books
67 Broadway
Asheville, NC 28801
828-253-0467

Manufactured in China

ISBN 13: 978-1-60059-345-1

For information about custom editions, special sales, premium and corporate purchases, please contact Sterling Special Sales Department at 800-805-5489 or specialsales@sterlingpub.com.

Contents

Introduction

Enameling is a decorative technique involving the fusion of glass and metal. Traditionally reserved for the production of jewelry and ornamental pieces, the art has a long and distinguished history. Over the past two decades, enameling has been taken up by artists working in a variety of media—a trend that has led to a blossoming of the material's expressive potential in new forms and applications.

Showcasing a diverse and talented group of international artists, this volume features the best enamel work being created today. A wide variety of pieces and approaches are included here, from jewelry to functional objects to installations, all of which demonstrate the current strength and breadth of the field.

Internationally and historically—unlike the areas of ceramics, textiles, painting, and woodworking—enameling has never been adopted as a major craft or art medium.

Enameling in the United States was rarely practiced in non-industrial applications until after World War II, when it became a favorite medium of hobbyists who were, for the most part, untrained in art principles and concepts. This popularity unfortunately brought with it a perception of the material as one not worthy of pursuit by serious artists. In Europe and Asia, the use of enamel has been relatively unbroken through the years. Until recently though, the material was used to produce fairly conventional forms and designs.

Amy Roper Lyons
Chambered Nautilus Pin #3 | 2007

While enameling has never been embraced as a major art form, it has held a constant position on the periphery, which may be due in part to the permanence of its colors and its intimate, gemlike qualities. It is a medium that requires expertise with two very different materials: enamel and metal. Enamel is essentially powdered glass specially formulated for applying to metal and for fusing at high temperatures. Enamel without metal is simply glass, while metal alone has a relatively limited palette. The combination and collaboration of the two materials is what makes enameled art unique, and the best artists use this relationship to its fullest, producing work that isn't possible in any other medium.

Many practitioners are more proficient with one material than the other. Some enamellists aren't skilled with metal, and this deficiency shows in relatively uninspired forms and settings. Conversely, many metalsmiths are uncomfortable with color, and their enamel work tends to be nearly monochromatic. The best enameled pieces take advantage of the strengths of each material. I looked for work that was excellent in both areas when choosing pieces for this book.

By far the largest number of pieces submitted fell into the category of personal adornment or jewelry objects. Enamel naturally lends itself to use in jewels in the traditional wearable sense, as Catherine Elizabeth Galloway's *Tile Earrings* (page 84), Amy Roper Lyons' *Chambered Nautilus Pin #3* (above), and Niki Ulehla's *Black Teeth* (page 122) beautifully demonstrate.

The traditional jewel form is also sometimes exploited by artists with a subversive intent, as in Sean Scully's *Navajo Yellowcake: Drum, Tower, Mineshaft* on page 137 (part of his very smart *Navajo Yellowcake* series) and the poignant *Endangered Species Carousel* bracelet by Kim Eric Lilot on page 51.

Within the category of adornment, a large contingent of pieces qualified as "gallery jewelry." Wearability isn't the focus of this type of work. Instead, many of these pieces are meant for viewing as art objects in a particular context. Susie Ganch's energetic untitled brooch (page 116), Kate Denslow's *Barnacle Ring* (page 22), and Emily Schuhmann's *Exponential Growth I* (page 364) are all examples of objects whose meanings are changed by their placement on the body.

Many enamellists are interested in making objects with aesthetic qualities that enhance the enjoyment of using them. In *Private Thought #1* (page 303), Ashley Pierce takes ordinary, commercially produced enamel plates and enamels them further to humorous effect. *The Birth of Venus* candlestick by Patricia Nelson (page 38), the *Red Top Teapot* by Maureen and Michael Banner (page 168), and *Leaf Cup* by Tamar De Vries Winter (below) are among the many pieces in this book that use enamel to enhance beautifully made metal structures that blur the line between functional and ceremonial work.

Recently, there have been both technical and conceptual breakthroughs in enameling that have made possible some wonderful sculptural pieces. Veleta Vancza's amazing glow-in-the-dark *Carbonado Series* (page 269), John Rais's cast-iron *Handbag Grouping* (page 179), and Yi Chen's salt-fired *Sea Creature #2* (page 23) all depart from traditional ways of thinking about enameling. Over the past 30 years, artists in a variety of media, including those working with vitreous enamel, have created larger environments and art installations. Successful examples of work in this vein can be found in this volume, including Maya Kini's untitled salt and enamel installation on page 63, Kim Lucci-Elbualy's powerful *The Spirit (LOVE)* on page 162, and Jessica Turrell's sensitive *Rememberings Installation* on page 32.

It is no coincidence that so many of the sculptural and jewelry pieces are white. In many cases the works can be viewed as an extension of the pristine contemporary art environment, a kind of flowing of the gallery walls onto the pieces themselves.

As I picked the wonderful images you see on these pages, I tried to include work that exhibited great technical virtuosity and work that was conceptually daring. Many of the chosen pieces exhibit both qualities. During the selection process, I was delighted to see how broad the scope of enameling has become and how quickly the field has developed in the last few decades. It is my hope that this book communicates and celebrates the brilliance and versatility of enamel and inspires artists interested in the material to continue working and innovating.

Sarah Perkins

Tamar De Vries Winter
Leaf Cup | 2008

David C. Freda

Shooting Stars
Orchid Brooch | 2003

8.9 X 10.2 X 5 CM

Fine silver, 24-karat yellow gold,
18-karat yellow gold, 14-karat
yellow gold, enamel, pearl; cast,
fabricated, granulation

PHOTO BY RALPH GABRINER

Tricia Lachowiec
Mentor | 2005
8.8 X 2.5 X 2.5 CM
14-karat gold, copper, enamel, sterling
silver; electroformed, oxidized
PHOTO BY DEAN POWELL

Patrizia Bonati

A3 (Ring) | 2003

2.7 X 0.7 CM

18-karat gold, enamel; chiseled, welded

PHOTO BY ARTIST

June Schwarcz
#2309 | 2006

16.5 X 16 X 15 CM

Copper foil, enamel,
gold; electroplated

PHOTOS BY LEE FATHERREE

Harlan W. Butt

Earth Beneath Our Feet: Maine Teapot #1 | 2007

15 X 15 X 13 CM

Fine silver, enamel, sterling silver; cloisonné, limoges

PHOTO BY RAFAEL MOLINA

John McVeigh
Lichen II, Brooch | 2007
5.2 X 4.1 X 0.8 CM
Sterling silver, copper, liquid enamel; pierced,
formed, torch fired, sifted, etched, fabricated
PHOTO BY ROBERT DIAMANTE

Jessica Calderwood
Flowers (Platter) | 2007
17.8 X 30.5 X 10.2 CM
Enamel, copper, brass; water-jet cut,
electroformed, limoges
PHOTO BY ARTIST

Joseph Handy
Fleece Pajamas Brooch | 2006
1.3 X 3.2 X 3.8 CM
Copper, sterling silver, microfleece,
enamel; formed, fabricated
PHOTOS BY ARTIST

Jennaca Leigh Davies

Teardrop Necklace | 2004

0.5 X 4.5 X 50 CM

Sterling silver, fine silver, enamel;
sifted, kiln fired, hand fabricated

PHOTO BY KATJA KULENKAMPFF

Yael Krakowski
Snake Bracelet—Blue | 2005
DIAMETER, 7 CM
Sterling silver, enamel, thread;
sifted, crocheted
PHOTO BY ARTIST

Mark Hartung
Untitled | 2006
20 X 38 X 38 CM
Copper, enamel; sifted
PHOTO BY ARTIST

Tan-Chi Chao
Dragee | 2001
19 X 8 X 8 CM
Copper, enamel; sifted,
painted, raised
PHOTO BY ARTIST

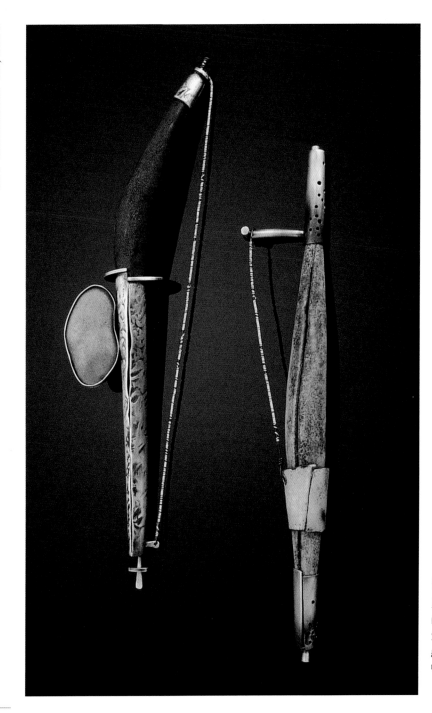

Felicia Szorad

Lure Brooch I and II | 2000

EACH, 15 X 4 X 1 CM

Sterling silver, copper, enamel, 14-karat gold; torch-fired limoges

PHOTO BY TAYLOR DABNEY

Sarah Perkins
Ochre Formation | 2008
22.8 X 8.9 X 8.9 CM
Copper, enamel; welded, fabricated
PHOTO BY ARTIST

Kate Denslow

Barnacle Ring | 2007

12.7 X 6.7 X 1.9 CM

Copper, sterling silver, enamel;
electroformed, sifted, painted,
etched, fabricated, prong set

PHOTO BY ARTIST

Yi Chen
Sea Creature #2 | 2008
7 X 11 X 11 CM
Copper, enamel; torch fired, raised
PHOTOS BY ARTIST

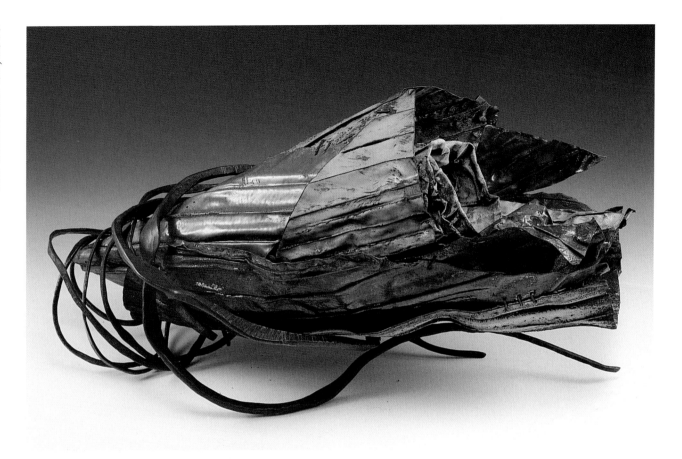

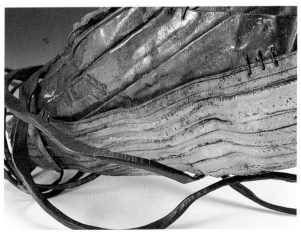

Mariah Tuttle

Oceana | 2006

16.5 X 38 X 20 CM

Copper, enamel; folded, forged, sifted, kiln fired

PHOTOS BY HELEN SHIRK

Kate Cathey

Stickpins | 2004

EACH, 12.8 X 4 X 4 CM

Copper, steel, enamel; fold formed,
chased, sifted, painted, over fired

PHOTO BY ROBERT DIAMANTE

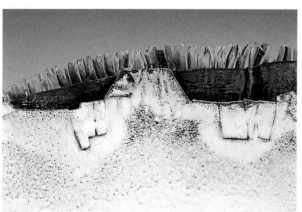

Mariah Tuttle

Sights in the City | 2006

13 X 28 X 28 CM

Copper, enamel, patina; sunk, textured,
etched, sifted, kiln fired

PHOTOS BY HELEN SHIRK

Hsiu-Chen Wang
Tree III | 2008
7.2 X 3.8 X 1.1 CM
Copper, enamel, sterling silver;
fold formed, wet inlaid, over fired,
fabricated, prong set
PHOTO BY IT PARK PHOTOGRAPHIC STUDIO

Jessica Kahle
Crystalline Blue-Grey Necklace | 2007
5 X 10 X 1 CM
Mica, enamel, silver
PHOTO BY ARTIST

Helen Carnac
Vitreous Enamel Vessels | 2008
LARGEST, 16 X 16 CM
Enamel, steel; wet processed,
sgraffito, kiln fired
PHOTO BY ARTIST

Bao-Guo Hong

Rice? | 2004

12 X 12 X 6 CM

Copper, enamel, found object; sifted

PHOTOS BY ARTIST

Amelia Toelke
Untitled | 2005
5.7 X 8.9 X 0.8 CM
Enamel, copper, sterling
silver; sifted, prong set
PHOTO BY ARTIST

My current work explores the process by which the viewing of family photographs and the articulation of associated memories can subtly take the place of true memories. This is a process that results in memories that represent the infinite layers of rememberings but rarely the pure unaltered experience. JESSICA TURRELL

Jessica Turrell
Rememberings Installation | 2007
EACH, 14.5 X 14.5 X 6 CM
Copper, enamel, photographs;
etched, sifted, stoned
PHOTOS BY ARTIST

Susie Ganch

Rest | 2007

50 X 56.3 X 26.3 CM

Steel, copper, enamel; fabricated

PHOTOS BY TAYLOR DABNEY

Veleta Vancza
Homage to Form/Confiscation of the Square | 2003
LARGEST, 40.6 X 40.6 X 25.4 CM
Copper, enamel; fused
PHOTOS BY ARTIST

Mirjam Hiller
Brooch | 2007
6 X 8 X 7 CM
Copper, sterling silver,
steel, enamel; rough fired
PHOTOS BY PETRA JASCHKE

I frequently use fantasy botanical forms as metaphors for human behaviors and characteristics, and this piece likens itself to a woman who uses every artifice to attract. Her hair is coiffed, lips painted, bosom thrust forward, and body scented as she attempts to draw attention to her 'finer' points.

LAURALEE HUTSON

Lauralee Hutson
Lure, Scent Vessel | 2008
65 X 37.5 X 25 CM
Enamel, copper, sterling silver; sifted, wet packed, fabricated, raised
PHOTOS BY LUMINA/FOX

Linda Darty
Untitled | 2008
6.4 X 12.7 X 0.6 CM
Sterling silver, enamel, 24-karat
gold, pearls; cloisonné
PHOTO BY ARTIST

Patricia Nelson
The Birth of Venus | 2008
38.1 X 22.9 X 22.9 CM
Sterling silver, copper, wood, enamel, rivets, bolts; sifted, kiln fired, cold connected
PHOTOS BY SERENA NANCARROW

Plants are my current fascination, as I have recently (and for the first time in my life) started gardening. Everything from root hairs to the glorious color of those long-awaited blossoms captivates me. The heightened colors in nature are great inspirations for the vivid possibilities of enamel.

PATRICIA NELSON

Rebecca Barton

Autumn is at Hund | 2007

2.5 X 27.9 X 5.1 CM

Copper, steel, enamel;
hydraulically pressed, sifted,
kiln fired, cold connected

PHOTOS BY ARTIST

Alisha Marie Boyd
Stacked Vessel | 2006
27 X 11 X 7 CM
Copper, enamel; deep
drawn, sifted, fused
PHOTO BY ARTIST

Carolyn Currin
Untitled Brooch | 2007
7.6 X 7.6 X 7.6 CM
Copper, enamel; sifted
PHOTO BY LINDA DARTY

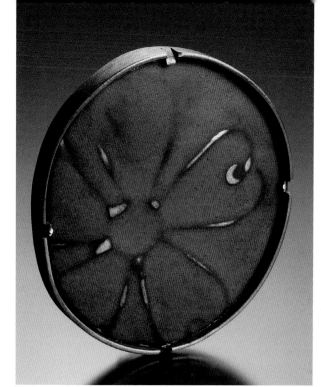

Marjorie Simon
Standing William Morris Brooch | 2006
5 X 7.6 X 0.6 CM
Enamel, copper, sterling silver, 18-karat gold;
embossed, sifted, tab set, kiln fired
PHOTO BY ROBERT DIAMANTE

Marlene True
Descansos #1 | 2007
4.5 X 6.5 X 0.6 CM
Copper, enamel, steel, 18-karat gold,
24-karat gold; sifted, underglazed,
textured, bezel set
PHOTO BY ARTIST

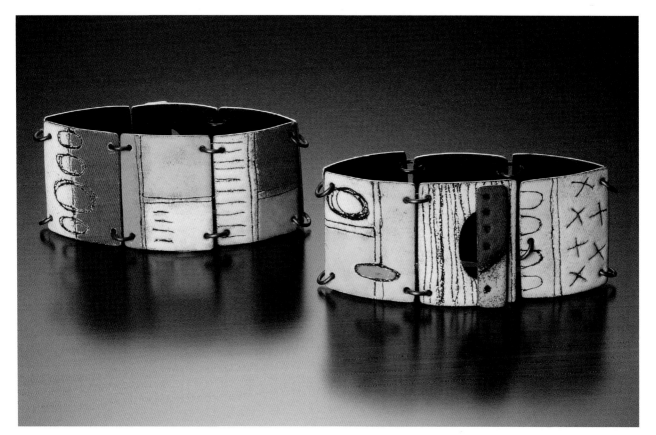

Angela Gerhard

Fozzy Bracelets | 2007

EACH, 3.2 X 19.1 X 0.6 CM

Copper, enamel; sifted,
sgraffito, etched

PHOTO BY ROBERT DIAMANTE

Jan Arthur Harrell

Entropy Houses | 2006

EACH, 15 X 10 X 15 CM

Copper, enamel, rocks, cork, brass, wire screen, bird nest, mirror, dryer lint, mica; sifted, stenciled, champlevé

PHOTOS BY JACK ZILKER

Karin Martin
8/29: Make Levees Not War | 2006
43.2 X 17.8 X 2.5 CM
Tin, copper, enamel, spray paint,
laser prints, recycled blue tarp, nylon
cord; fabricated, sifted, kiln fired
PHOTO BY JACK ZILKER

Viktoria Münzker-Ferus
Enamel as Pigment 03—Brooch | 2006
3 X 5.6 X 1.2 CM
Brass, silver, enamel, polyester resin; cast
PHOTO BY ARTIST

This piece consists of gel capsules con-
taining enamels labeled with their
'names' and the manufacturer's number,
each sorted by color and placed in antique
glass medicine bottles. The piece contrasts
the hopefulness of medicine and the heal-
ing power of color with the paradox of the
toxic nature of enamel in its unfired state.

SUSAN KINGSLEY

Susan Kingsley
Rx | 2000
11.5 X 25 X 8 CM
Raw enamel, gel caps, glass
jars, mirror
PHOTO BY ROBERT NEIMY

My inspiration comes from Victorian mourning symbolism and from modern advances in medical science. The animals used by science for studies that allow human life to be extended are creatures I find worth memorializing in my work. The MRL mouse that doesn't scar, the self-regenerating salamander—these and other medical marvels all are fair play in my attempts to find beauty in animals that are often associated with feelings of disgust. EMILY BUTE

Emily Bute

To Preserve: Tardigrade | 2007
DIAMETER, 25 CM
Copper, enamel, fine silver,
24-karat gold; cloisonné
PHOTO BY ARTIST

Miel-Margarita Paredes

Deliberate | 2004

33 X 30 X 30 CM

Copper, enamel, brass, patina;
raised, chased, welded, sifted

PHOTO BY STEPHEN FUNK

Lezlie Jane

Running Scared | 1991

45.7 X 91.4 CM

Enamel, steel; cut, filed, welded, sprayed, kiln fired, sifted

PHOTO BY KEN WAGNER

Why is it the gentle ones we go after? LEZLIE JANE

Kim Eric Lilot

Endangered Species Carousel | 2006

2.5 X 24.5 X 0.5 CM

18-karat white gold, 18-karat green
gold, Burmese ruby cabochons,
enamel; hand fired

PHOTOS BY DOUG YAPLE

Maya Kini
Breaking the Ranks | 2008
61 X 91.4 X 1.9 CM
Steel, enamel; sifted, sugar fired
PHOTOS BY ARTIST

Jonathan Wahl
Lark Ring | 2006
2.5 X 2.5 X 3.8 CM
14-karat gold, enamel; champlevé

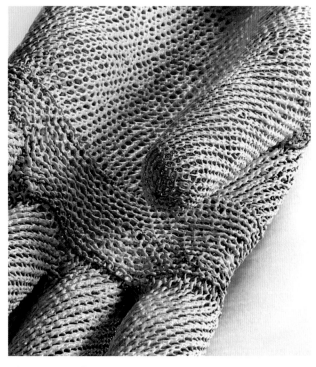

Shu-Wan Chu
Right Hand | 2008

25 X 9 X 5 CM

Copper wire, enamel, paper,
plastics; crocheted, sifted

PHOTOS BY ARTIST

Stephanie Tomczak
Angelito, a Mourning Portrait | 2006
3.8 X 2.5 X 1.1 CM
Copper, enamel, 18-karat
gold; electroformed
PHOTO BY KEN YANOVIAK

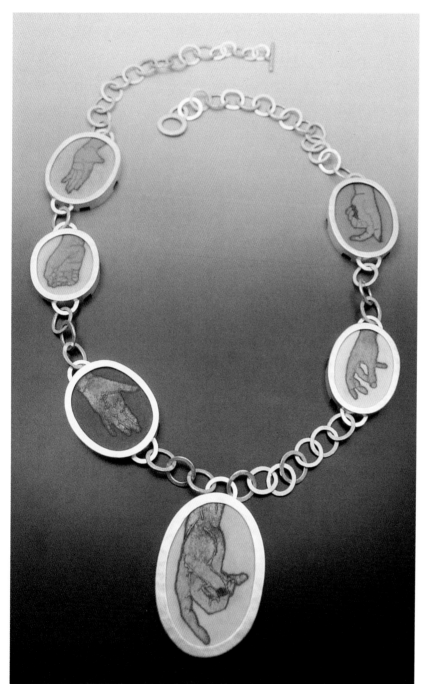

Emily Watson

Beyond the Lover's Eye:
Six Hands Necklace | 2005

42 X 6.3 X 1 CM

Sterling silver, copper, enamel; acid etched,
wet packed, painted, kiln fired, bezel set

PHOTO BY ARTIST

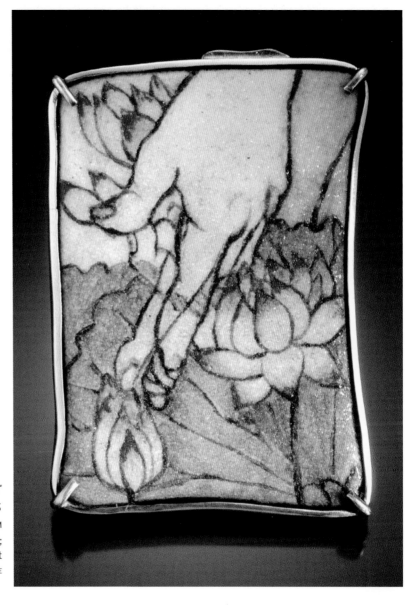

The brooches in this series lend a visual context to human desires and the vulnerability of women to notions of idealized beauty that are often distorted by cultural sensibilities. For example, the purpose of Chinese foot binding—a painful, crippling practice—was to create the visual effect of delicate lotus blossoms. MI-SOOK HUR

Mi-Sook Hur
Deformed Beauty III: Lotus' Lust | 2005
4.5 X 6.3 X 0.5 CM
Sterling silver, copper, enamel;
painted, prong set
PHOTO BY ROBERT DIAMANTE

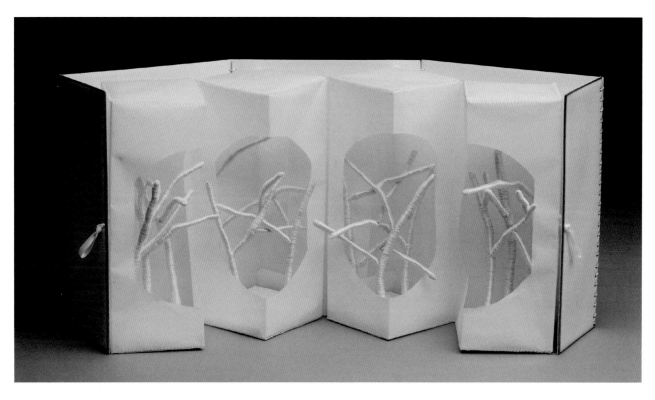

Maria Papalia
Sanctuary I | 2007
17 X 13 X 13 CM
Clay, paper, thread, copper,
enamel; sifted, kiln fired
PHOTOS BY ARTIST

Kye-Yeon Son
Winter Scene | 2006
LARGEST, 7.5 X 27 X 16 CM
Copper, enamel; soldered,
electroformed, sifted
PHOTO BY GEORGE GEORGAKAKOS

Maya Kini
Assorted Drains:
Brooch and Ring | 2008
RING, 3.2 X 6.2 X 3.2 CM
BROOCHES, 3.2 X 3.2 X 0.6 CM
Sterling silver, enamel;
sifted, sugar fired, bezel set
PHOTOS BY ARTIST

Joshua R. Jackson
Aurothioglycolanide Separator | 2004
18 X 23 X 15 CM
Copper, enamel, latex tube, found
object; raised, sifted

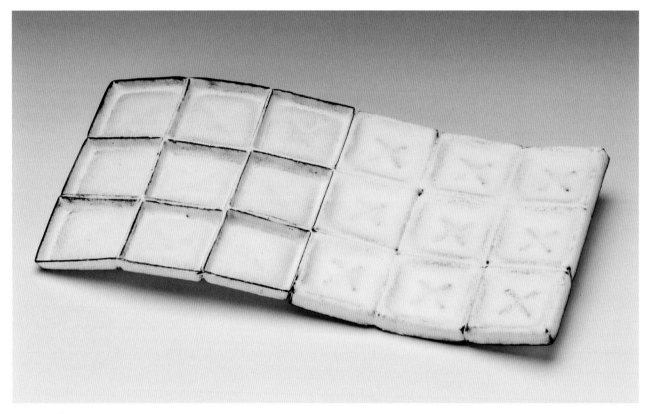

Yung-Ching Lai
Model Inside, Model Flank | 2006
4 X 20 X 10 CM
Copper, enamel; sifted, sandblasted
PHOTO BY K'UNLUNG CAI

Maya Kini
Untitled | 2007
EACH BLOCK, 26 X 15 X 15 CM
Salt licks, copper, enamel
PHOTOS BY ARTIST

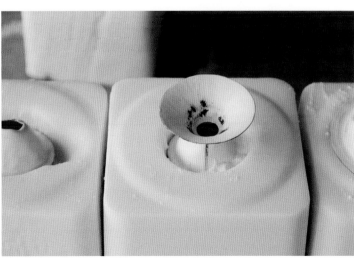

Mana Kehr
Egg Cups and Napkin Rings | 2008
EACH, 4 X 5 X 5 CM
Sterling silver, enamel, cord; wound,
hammered, knotted, furnace burned
PHOTOS BY STEFANIE RAHMSTORF

Jessica Schlachter-Townsend
Vessel 82907 | 2007
43.2 X 6.4 X 7.6 CM
Copper, enamel; sprayed, torch
fired, oxyacetylene welded
PHOTOS BY ARTIST

Vivian Stillwell

Earth Elements I | 2007

22 X 22 X 2.5 CM

Copper, enamel, oxides;
painted, reduction fired

PHOTO BY JANE BEISER

Jessica Kahle
Pinwheel Brooch | 2007
9 X 9 X 2.5 CM
Mica, enamel, 18-karat
gold; fabricated

Deborrah Daher

Orange Desert Brooch | 2002

7 X 5.9 X 0.4 CM

Fine silver, sterling silver, enamel;
sifted, kiln fired, reverse prong set

PHOTO BY RALPH GABRINER

Fabrizio Tridenti
Contro-Verso | 2007
4.7 X 3.2 X 3.4 CM
Silver, enamel; soldered, fired
PHOTO BY ARTIST

June Schwarcz
#2326 | 2007
19 X 21.5 X 13.3 CM
Foil, enamel; electroplated
PHOTO BY LEE FATHERREE

Dorothea Hosom

Untitled Brooch #1 | 2005

8.7 X 1.3 X 0.3 CM

Silver, gold, enamel, copper; wet
packed, stoned, bezel set

PHOTO BY ARTIST

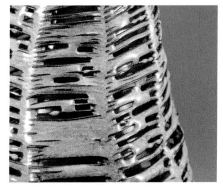

Alisha Marie Boyd
Untitled | 2006
26 X 11.5 X 9 CM
Copper, enamel;
sifted, torch fired
PHOTOS BY ARTIST

Yuh-Shyuan Chen
Water Inside | 2008
1.5 X 8.5 X 7.5 CM
Copper, enamel, black lead; sifted
PHOTOS BY ARTIST

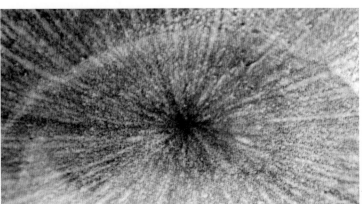

Hiu-ning Chuang
Decorated Object | 2008

30 X 25 X 2 CM

Sterling silver, enamel;
sifted, granulation

PHOTOS BY ARTIST

Diane Echnoz Almeyda
Trapped #1 | 2007
4.3 X 8.1 X 8.1 CM
Fine silver, enamel;
filigree, plique-à-jour
PHOTOS BY ARTIST

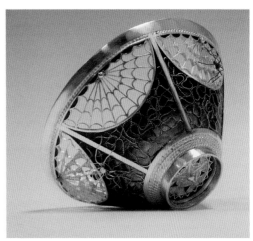

Kathleen Rearick
Untitled | 2008
7.5 X 2.5 X 0.8 CM
Sterling silver, enamel, decal;
fabricated, oxidized, limoges
PHOTO BY ARTIST

Anke AMO Akerboom
Alopecúrus pranténsis | 1991

7 X 2 X 2 CM

Container for perfume, 24-karat
gold-plated sterling silver,
enamel; fabricated, plique-à-jour

PHOTOS BY ARTIST

Gillie Hoyte Byrom
Henry VIII 1537, After
Hans Holbein the Younger | 2007
13.9 X 7.7 CM
Enamel, 18-karat gold, gold paste; shaped,
engraved, painted, kiln fired, stoned, polished
PHOTOS BY COLIN RILEY

The client for this commissioned piece
chose the subject himself, requiring me to
study the work of Hans Holbein the Younger
and to create a portrait of Henry VIII in
Holbein's style. Translating Holbein's medium of
oil paint into vitreous enamel made this the
most technically challenging miniature I've ever
produced. The piece combines engraving with
foils, gold wire, gold dust, liquid gold, and
vitreous enamel. The layered effect gives the
figure a three-dimensional quality while
allowing light to play over the surface and
enhance the features. GILLIE HOYTE BYROM

Errico Cassar
Untitled | 2001
1.2 X 4.5 X 6 CM
22-karat gold, garnets, enamel, gold foil;
sifted, kiln fired, carborundum stone
ground, sanded, claw set
PHOTO BY ARTIST

Truike Verdegaal

Amulet por Marzee | 1993

3.5 X 7 X 3.5 CM

Gold, silver, jade, enamel, glass, Delftware; fabricated, fired

PHOTO BY GERHARD JAEGER

This amulet was especially made for Marie José van den Hout, owner of the Gallery Marzee, Nijmegen, The Netherlands. The piece is a protecting eye that has her initials enameled in the iris. She can carry (and feel) it in her pocket. The thorn on the left side reminds her to be cautious of danger, while the rose on the right side represents the bright side of life. And, of course, the pieces of Delftware on gold chain will bring her prosperity. TRUIKE VERDEGAAL

Jenny Edlund
Amor Fati Series: Ring | 2004
4.5 X 3 X 2 CM
Sterling silver, enamel, freshwater
pearl, raw tourmaline; gilded
PHOTO BY ARTIST

Irakli Bolgashvili

Brooch | 2008

6 X 4.5 CM

Silver, enamel, pearl, cubic
zirconia; gilded, cloisonné

PHOTO BY TAMAR BOTCHORISHVILI

**Joanne S. Conant
Margarete Seeler**

The Nine Muses | 2003

2 X 16.5 X 17.7 CM

18-karat gold, enamel;
champlevé, cloisonné

PHOTOS BY BRAD STANTON

Catherine Elizabeth Galloway

Tile Earrings | 2007

EACH, 2 X 2 CM

18-karat gold, diamonds,
enamel; champlevé, pave set

PHOTO BY HAP SAKWA

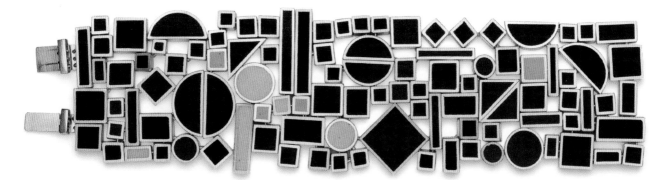

John Iversen
Cityscape Revisited | 2006
18.4 X 5.1 X 0.3 CM
18-karat gold, enamel; fabricated
PHOTO BY ROBERT HENSLEIGH

Patrizia Bonati
C1 (Brooch) | 2003
6 X 1.2 CM
18-karat gold, enamel; chiseled
PHOTO BY ARTIST

Ralph Bakker
Grote Krokodil | 2004
30 X 15 CM
Gold, silver, enamel; sifted,
kiln fired, assembled
PHOTO BY ARTIST

Joan MacKarell

Wavy Agate Necklace | 2006

EACH BEAD, 3 X 0.5 CM

Silver, gold, enamel, agate beads;
repoussé, wet packed

PHOTO BY FULL FOCUS

For many years I've been exploring the ways in which found objects invoke or stir up memories. I've also been deriving many of the colors I use from metallic oxides, by bleeding the colors out of the host metal into the enamel during firing. Surfaces are usually matte to help with the subtle effects. GLENICE LESLEY MATTHEWS

Glenice Lesley Matthews
Skimming Pebble I | 2007
4.5 X 6 X 1 CM
Fine silver, metallic oxides, enamels; granulation, fabricated, raised, matte finish
PHOTO BY ARTIST

Kate Denslow

Tunicate Necklace | 2007

48.3 X 4.5 X 2.5 CM

Copper, 24-karat gold, enamel; electroformed, sifted

PHOTOS BY ARTIST

Aran Galligan
Flora Series: Circle Pin | 2007
4 X 4 X 2.5 CM
Sterling silver, copper, enamel;
repoussé, sifted, over fired, prong set
PHOTO BY STEVE MANN

Sofia Björkman
Grandmother | 2004
2 X 2 X 4 CM
Silver, enamel; burned, cast
PHOTO BY ARTIST

Connie Jan
Cluster No. 1 | 2007
4.5 X 6 X 1.5 CM
Copper, enamel;
electroformed, sifted

PHOTO BY ARTIST

Jennifer Carland
Untitled | 2004
26 X 11 X 9 CM
Copper, enamel, patina
PHOTOS BY ARTIST

Shasha Higby
Clam | 2007
12 X 20 X 12 CM
Copper, enamel; form
folded, sifted, torch fired
PHOTO BY ARTIST

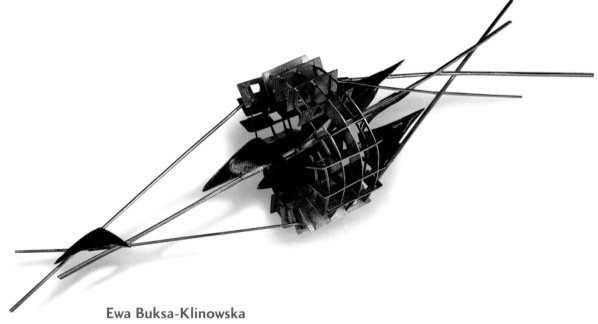

Ewa Buksa-Klinowska
Fire | 2007
7 X 16 X 8 CM
Gold, sterling silver, enamel;
basse taille, hand fabricated
PHOTO BY ARTIST

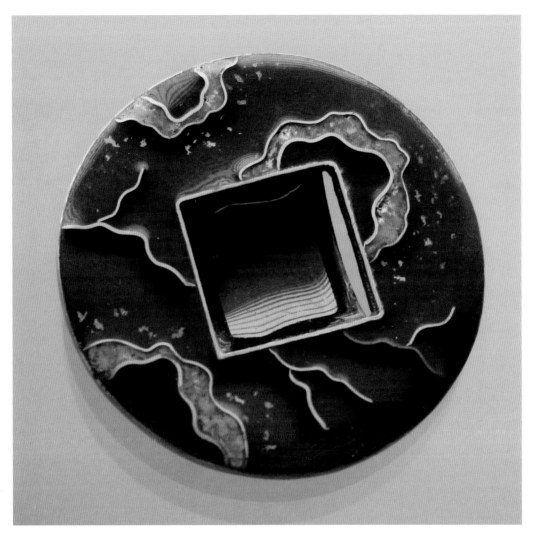

Minna Karhu
Untitled Brooch | 2006
3.9 X 3.9 X 0.7 CM
Copper, enamel, gold; gilded,
cloisonné, kiln fired
PHOTO BY ARTIST

Seongbun Kim

The Annual Ring | 2006

4 X 4.5 X 3.5 CM

Sterling silver, copper, enamel;
etched, sifted, kiln fired, bezel set

PHOTOS BY KEN COX

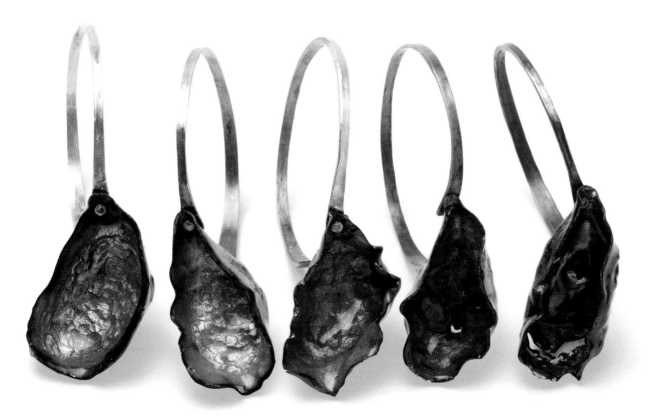

Jessie Yeager
Untitled | 2007
7 X 3.8 X 7.5 CM
Sterling silver, copper, enamel;
die formed, chased, forged
PHOTOS BY JOSEPH BYRD

Demitra Thomloudis

Untitled | 2007

16 X 2 X 2 CM

Fine silver, sterling silver, pearls,
enamel, gold; cast, sifted, fabricated

PHOTOS BY ARTIST

Marybeth Bent

Growth Shoulder Brooch | 2007

16 X 14 X 10 CM

Sterling silver, copper, boxwood,
enamel; painted, torch fired

PHOTO BY BIANCA GAMBARDELLA

María del Pilar Zornosa

*Sterling Silver Tiara with
Enameled Flowers* | 2007

5 X 15 X 2.5 CM

Sterling silver, enamel; forged,
sifted, cold connected

PHOTO BY ARTIST

Barbara Minor

Zinnia—Pin/Pendant | 2007

3.8 X 7.6 X 0.6 CM

Enamel, copper, sterling silver,
glass, brass; sifted, inlaid, fabricated

PHOTO BY RALPH GABRINER

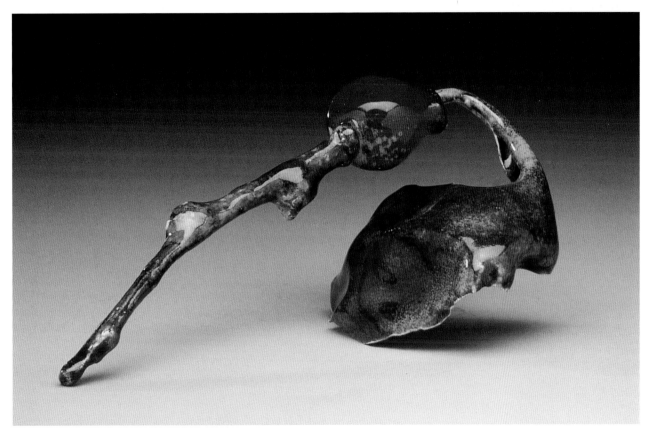

Yoshiko Yamamoto

Object: Cycle of Life (Metamorphosis) | 2005

4.7 X 10.2 X 4 CM

Sterling silver, fine silver, enamel; cast,
forged, fabricated, sifted, kiln fired

PHOTO BY DEAN POWELL

Karen Lee

The Vibrant Symbiont | 2006

11.4 X 32.4 X 10.5 CM

Copper, enamel, colored pencils,
patina; raised, sifted, pierced, fabricated

PHOTO BY HELEN SHIRK

Natalya Pinchuk
Growth Series: Brooch | 2005
6.5 X 7.5 X 7.5 CM
Copper, enamel, plastic, stainless
steel; electroformed, sifted
PHOTO BY ARTIST

Marianne Contreras

Numnums | 2007

105 X 1.3 CM

Copper, enamel, stainless steel, sterling
silver; electroformed, sifted

PHOTO BY KEN YANOVIAK

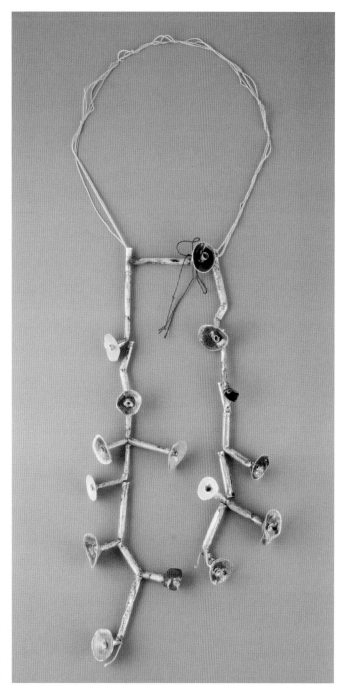

Venetia Moushey Dale
Blooms on Gold | 2006
101.6 X 15.2 X 1.9 CM
Fine silver, enamel, silk thread;
hand fabricated, over fired
PHOTO BY ARTIST

Natalya Pinchuk
Growth Series: Brooch | 2005
14 X 8 X 8 CM
Copper, enamel, plastic, stainless
steel; electroformed, sifted
PHOTO BY ARTIST

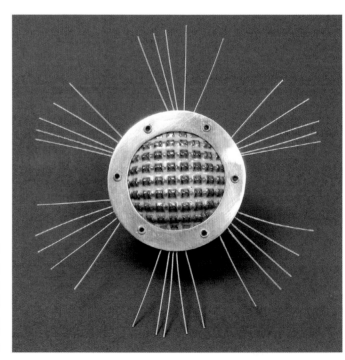

Jill Leventon
Brooch | 2008
DIAMETER, 9 CM
Copper, sterling silver, nylon-covered
wire, enamel; sifted, kiln fired,
corrugated, press formed, riveted
PHOTO BY RUSSELL PARRY

Veleta Vancza
Target Re-Formed | 2003
27.9 X 27.9 X 20.3 CM
Copper, enamel; fused
PHOTOS BY ARTIST

Roxanne Watts

Brooch Series | 2007

EACH, 6.5 X 5 X 0.3 CM

Fine silver, sterling silver, mild
steel, enamel; cloisonné, sandblasted,
oil quenched, formed

PHOTO BY ARTIST

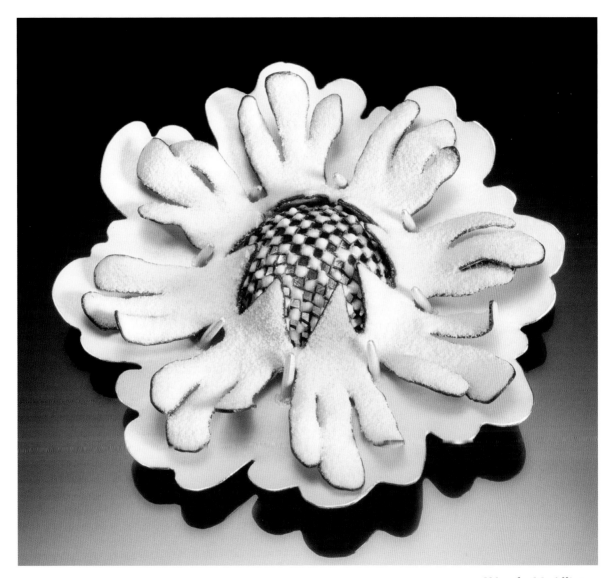

Wendy McAllister

Snow (Brooch) | 2007

7.5 X 7.5 X 2 CM

Copper, copper mesh, sterling
silver, enamel; sugar fired,
prong set, depletion gilded

PHOTO BY RALPH GABRINER

Liz Schock
White Lantern Bracelet | 2007
19.1 X 5.1 X 2.5 CM
Copper, enamel, satin ribbon; kiln fired
PHOTO BY DEAN POWELL

Meagan Clark
Untitled | 2007
22 X 18 X 1 CM
Sterling silver, copper, liquid
enamel; wire wrapped
PHOTO BY LINDA DARTY

Jessica Schlachter-Townsend
Form Through Fire: 122107 | 2007
226.1 X 22.9 X 25.4 CM
Copper, porcelain enamel; sprayed,
torch fired, oxyacetylene welded
PHOTOS BY ARTIST

Lori Hawke-Ramin
Drawer Pull Necklaces | 2007
EACH, 9.5 X 4 X 0.5 CM
Sterling silver, enamel, nylon cord
PHOTO BY PETER TURNER AND ARTIST

Masako Onodera
Fireworks | 2007
7.5 X 16.5 X 5 CM
Copper, enamel; sifted, kiln fired, etched
PHOTO BY ARTIST

Susie Ganch

Untitled (Brooch) | 2008

12.5 X 12.5 X 5 CM

Sterling silver, stainless steel,
copper, enamel; fabricated

PHOTO BY ARTIST

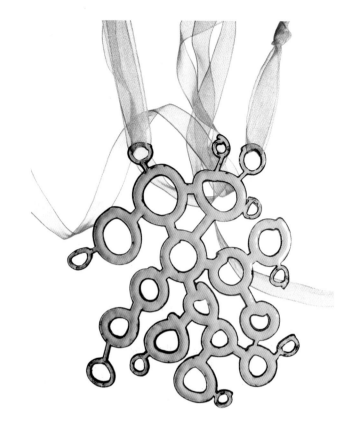

Roberta Bernabei Shaw
Untitled | 2005
0.2 X 12 X 12 CM
Copper, organza, enamel; photo-etched

Jimin Park
Untitled | 2008
28 X 16 X 5 CM
Copper, enamel, plastic beads; sifted

Ingrid Römmich

Ring Without a Diamond | 2004

EACH, 3 X 2.5 X 1 CM

Sterling silver, enamel; melted

PHOTO BY ARTIST

Dubbelop

Snow White, Pendant 01 | 2004

3 X 4 X 0.8 CM

Titanium, enamel; kiln fired

PHOTO BY JAN MATTESIUS

Alissa Lamarre
Soft Growth Series, #2 | 2008
46 X 18 CM
Copper, enamel, felt; sifted, sugar fired
PHOTO BY ARTIST

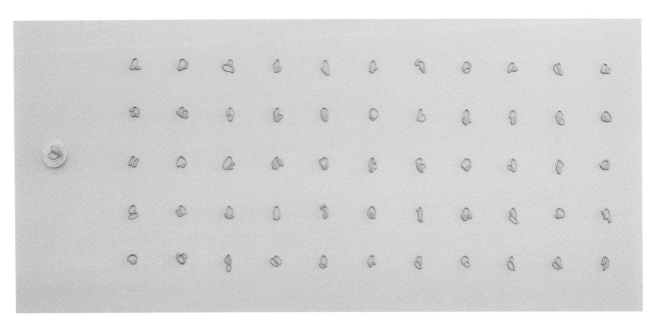

Lynn Batchelder

Objects to Incorporate Into
Your Everyday Life | 2007

WALL INSTALLATION, 63 X 140 CM
BROOCH, 6.5 X 6.5 X 2 CM

Sterling silver, spring steel,
copper, enamel; torch fired

PHOTOS BY ARTIST

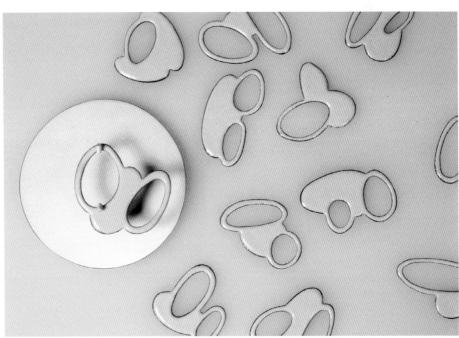

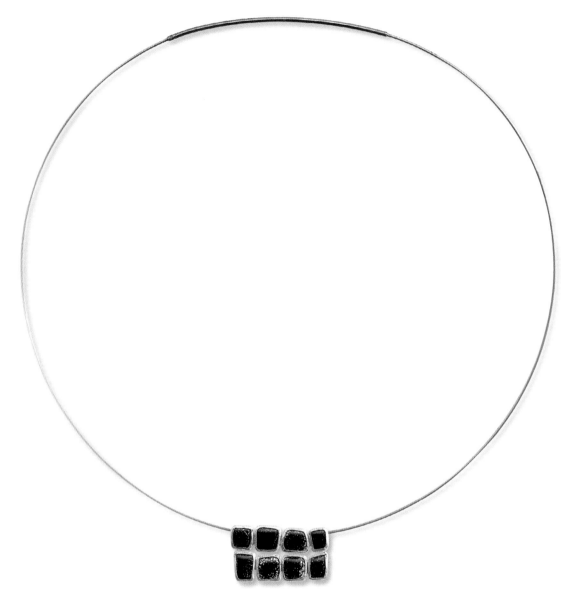

Niki Ulehla

Black Teeth | 2006

1.6 X 2.8 X 0.5 CM

18-karat gold, 22-karat gold,
enamel, copper; torch fired, bezel set

PHOTO BY ARTIST

Yung-Ching Lai
Assembly—Triangle | 2006
7.5 X 7.5 X 6 CM
Copper, enamel; sifted, sandblasted
PHOTOS BY ARTIST

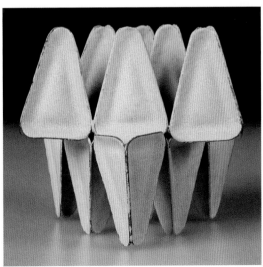

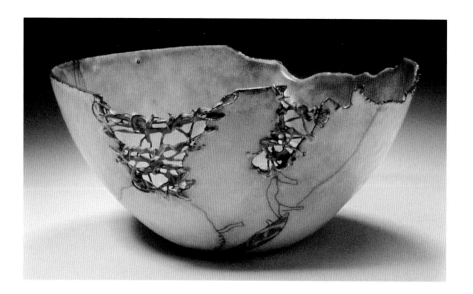

Judy Stone
Burnt Offering: XVI | 2004
16.5 X 7.6 CM
Copper, gold foil, enamel; fabricated,
cut, riveted, sewn, sgraffito, sifted,
limoges, satin finished
PHOTOS BY RALPH GABRINER

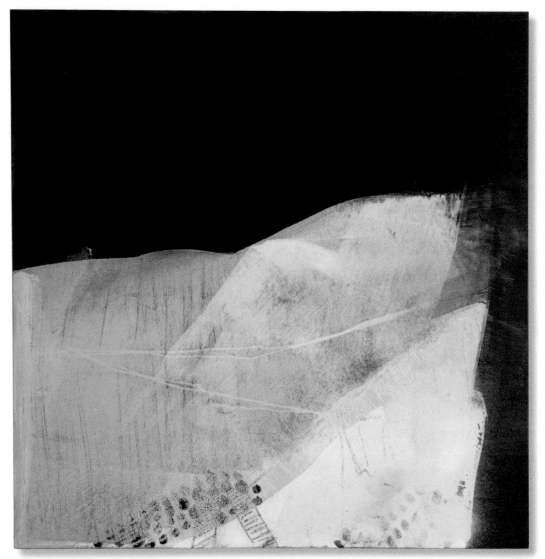

Helen Elliott
Journal 7 | 2007
30.5 X 30.5 X 3.8 CM
Porcelain enamel, jewelry enamel, steel,
wood; painted, sifted, mounted
PHOTO BY GREG STALEY

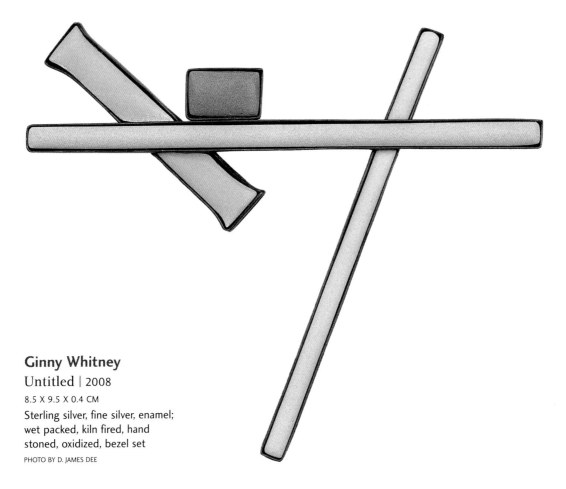

Ginny Whitney
Untitled | 2008

8.5 X 9.5 X 0.4 CM

Sterling silver, fine silver, enamel;
wet packed, kiln fired, hand
stoned, oxidized, bezel set

PHOTO BY D. JAMES DEE

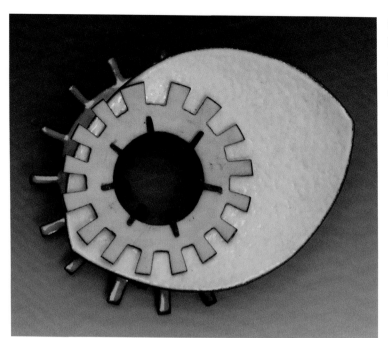

Carolyn Currin
Untitled Brooch | 2006
5.1 X 7.6 X 0.6 CM
Copper, enamel; sifted
PHOTO BY LINDA DARTY

Ann Schmalwasser
Winter, Brooch | 2006
8 X 10.4 X 0.7 CM
Copper, enamel
PHOTO BY ARTIST

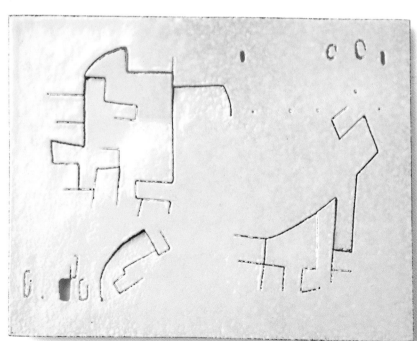

Beate Klockmann

Limewire | 2007

35 X 25 X 0.5 CM

Enamel, copper tube, gold; fabricated

PHOTO BY ARTIST

Joanna Gollberg
Like Amy, but I Didn't Know It | 2006
7.6 X 3.8 X 0.3 CM
Steel, enamel; wet packed,
sifted, kiln fired
PHOTO BY ARTIST

Katy Bergman Cassell
Lost in Iraq | 2004

275 X 183 X 92 CM

Porcelain enamel, jewelry enamel,
steel, copper, clay, conté crayon;
sifted, etched, image transfer

PHOTOS BY ARTIST

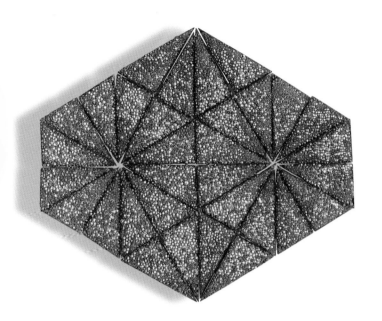

Joan Parcher

Phosphene Brooches | 2007

EACH, 7 X 6.5 X 1 CM

Reflective glass, enamel, copper,
sterling silver; sifted, kiln fired, fabricated

PHOTO BY JAMES BEARDS PHOTOGRAPHY

Kim Lucci-Elbualy
The Body (Faith) | 2005
170 X 32 X 5.5 CM
Copper, enamel; die formed,
welded, sifted, brushed, torch fired
PHOTOS BY ARTIST

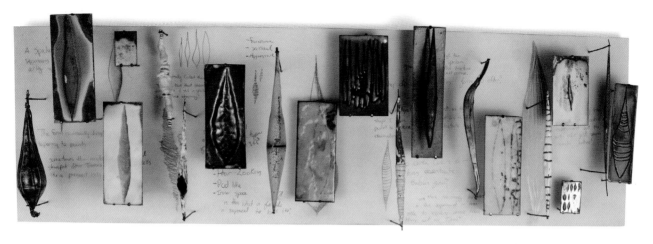

Kat Cole
Untitled: Experiments in Enameling | 2007
91.4 X 30.5 X 3.8 CM
Enamel, steel, wood, copper
PHOTOS BY ARTIST

Jill Baker Gower
Reflection #1 | 2006

13.3 X 8.9 X 7.6 CM

Copper, enamel, acrylic mirror, silicone
rubber; cast, raised, sifted, fabricated

PHOTO BY ARTIST

IN EATING DESSERT IT IS CUSTOM TO DIP THE BOWL OF THE SPOON TOWARD YOU AND EAT FROM THE END.

HELD IN THE RIGHT HAND LIKE A FORK

IN EATING DESSERT IT IS CUSTOM TO DIP THE BOWL OF THE SPOON TOWARD YOU AND EAT FROM THE END.

Sarah Jane Ross

A Silver Dessert Spoon with the Necessary Instructions for a Faultless Performance at the Dinner Table, and Training Spoon | 2002

EACH, ?? X 4 5 X 0.1 CM

Sterling silver, copper, enamel; photo etched, sifted, fabricated

PHOTO BY STUDIO INGOT

Elizabeth Turrell
Universal Declaration of Human Rights
Series: Red Cross | 2008
6 X 6 CM
Enamel, copper; etched
PHOTOS BY ARTIST

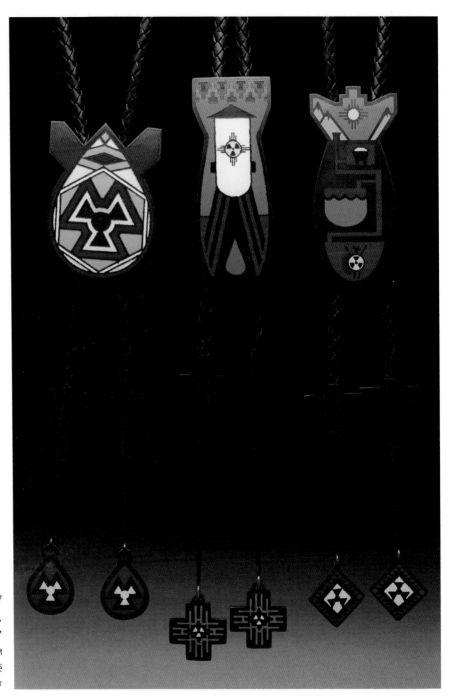

> I search out controversial issues—subjects that fascinate me—and encode the frequently violent nature of those subjects through the use of juxtapositions, abstraction, and obtuse symbolism.
>
> SEAN W. SCULLY

Sean W. Scully
Navajo Yellowcake: Drum, Tower, Mineshaft | 2007
TALLEST, 24.1 X 3.8 X 1.3 CM
Copper, enamel, leather; champlevé
PHOTO BY ARTIST

Karl A. Stupka
Don't Give Your Time to the Machine | 2008
30.5 X 40.6 X 15.2 CM
Copper, found objects, enamel; sifted
PHOTOS BY LINDA DARTY

Nisa Blackmon

The Evolution of Flying Things | 2006

GROUP, 4 X 50 X 30 CM

Copper, enamel, model airplane
ceramic decals; folded, sifted, kiln fired

PHOTOS BY ARTIST

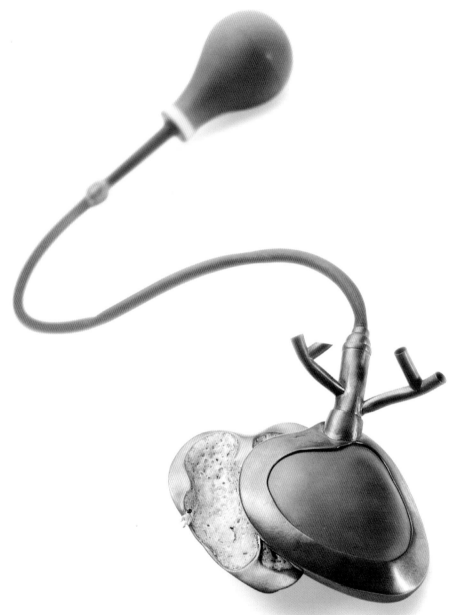

An-Chi Wang
Trying Hard to Live | 2006
6.5 X 8 X 60 CM
Copper, elastomeric, enamel; pressed
PHOTOS BY ARTIST

Marcela M. McLean
Bleeding Hearts | 2007
30 X 17 CM
Wood, enamel, copper, oxides; hand painted
PHOTO BY ARTIST

Anita Van Doorn
Respirator | 2007
13.5 X 12 X 7 CM
Copper, brass, enamel, patina, leather; formed, soldered, cloisonné, riveted
PHOTO BY ARTIST

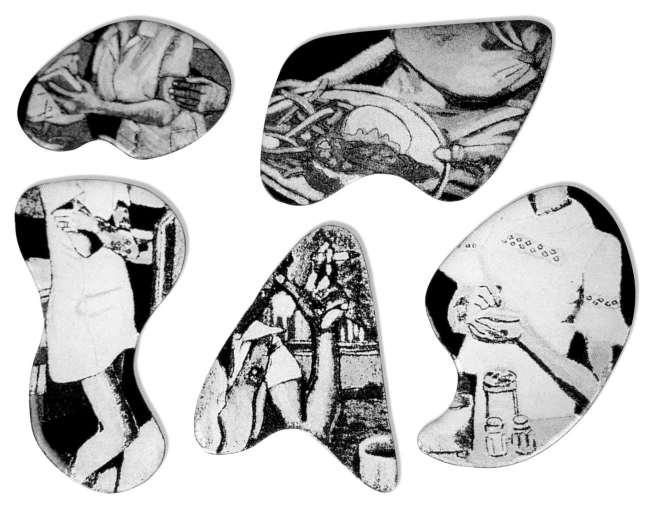

Laura Fortune

Diner Series | 2004

LARGEST, 7 X 5.1 X 2 CM

Copper, enamel; grisaille

PHOTO BY ARTIST

Portrait eyes, also called lover's eyes, date back to the late 1700s. At this time, supposedly, the Prince of Wales and his mistress, Mrs. Fitzherbert, wanted to exchange portrait miniatures but wanted to do so discreetly. To solve their problem, the court miniaturist suggested painting eye miniatures—portraits of only the two lovers' eyes. JULIA FLUKER

Julia Fluker for Maenad Design
Lover's Eyes for Alan Greenspan | 2007
EACH, 2 X 2 X 0.3 CM
18-karat gold, diamonds, enamel;
painted, kiln fired
PHOTO BY JAY BACHEMIN

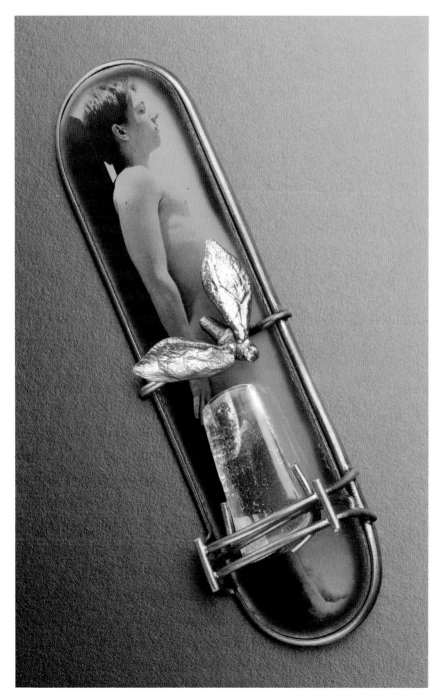

Just like a fossilized insect trapped forever in amber, my piece allows the viewer to reflect on a feeling of eternal stasis. This piece incorporates a self-portrait, which captures a single second in time, much like the amber, preserving a moment that may be reflected on forever. ANDREW L. KUEBECK

Andrew L. Kuebeck
In One Moment . . .
(Self Portrait) | 2007
10 X 4 X 2 CM
Copper, enamel, photo, sterling silver, amber, patina; fabricated, basket set, processed
PHOTO BY KEITH MEISER

144

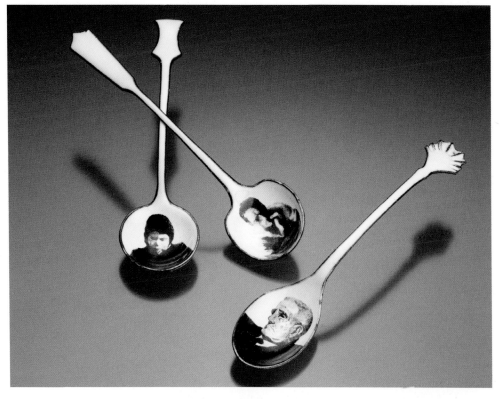

Joseph M. Pillari
Unknown Momento Spoons | 2008
EACH, 16 X 3 X 3 CM
Copper, enamel; sifted,
kiln fired, limoges
PHOTOS BY KEN YANOVIAK

Jessica Calderwood
Something in the Air (Platter) | 2007
17.8 X 30.5 X 10.2 CM
Enamel, copper, brass; die formed,
water jet cut, electroformed, limoges

Sherida Wank
Ladies' Man | 2006
14 X 7.6 X 0.5 CM
Copper, enamel; sifted, kiln fired
PHOTO BY BILL LEMKE

Genava Gisondi
They Work Hard for the Money | 2007
EACH, 9 X 9 X 0.3 CM
Copper, enamel, photo transfer
decal, synthetic chest hair wig,
epoxy; sifted, kiln fired, glued
PHOTO BY KEN YANOVIAK

Amanda Fisher
Plique-à-Jour Smiley Face | 2006
5.1 X 3.5 X 0.4 CM
Sterling silver, fine silver,
enamel, sapphire, black diamond;
filigree, plique-à-jour, bezel set
PHOTO BY JUSTIN FISHER

Nikki Majajas
Our Ladies of Sorrows
Series: Anna Nicole | 2007
12 X 7 X 0.5 CM
Tombak, plastic and metal rosary
beads, enamel; sifted, etched
PHOTO BY ARTIST

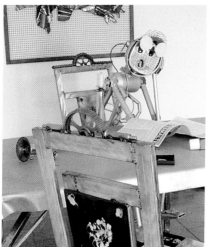

**Nubrae's Artists: Barbara Altstadt,
Dirceu Americo, Mirthes Bernardes,
Maria P. Carvalho, and Cid Freitas**
Lost Laid Off | 2006
250 X 200 X 200 CM
Enamel, copper, steel, found
objects; constructed, sifted
PHOTOS BY MARIA CARVALHO

Sally Aplin
Five | 2007
EACH, 13 X 31 X 10 CM
Copper foil, wood,
enamel; sifted
PHOTO BY PETER APLIN

Ashley N. Pierce
Private Thought #2 | 2008
26 X 3.5 CM
Commercial steel enamelware,
liquid enamel; sgraffito
PHOTO BY LINDA DARTY

Bronwyn Jayne Pressey
Well Done, Keep It Down | 2006
EACH, 2 X 1.5 X 3 CM
Fine silver, sterling silver,
enamel; cloisonné, bezel set
PHOTO BY THERESE DEVILLIERS

Beate Eismann
Busts | 2006
EACH PENDANT, 6 X 7.5 X 0.6 CM
Copper, enamel, German silver, precious
stones; sawed, soldered, set
PHOTO BY ARTIST

Demitra Thomloudis
Resist All Things
Sweet and Delicious | 2007
7 X 3 X 3 CM
Sterling silver, enamel;
sugar fired, bezel set, cast
PHOTOS BY ARTIST

Suzanne Kustner
Atkins-Approved Candy | 2000
EACH, 3 X 3 X 2 CM
Copper, liquid enamel; sifted
PHOTO BY HAP SAKWA

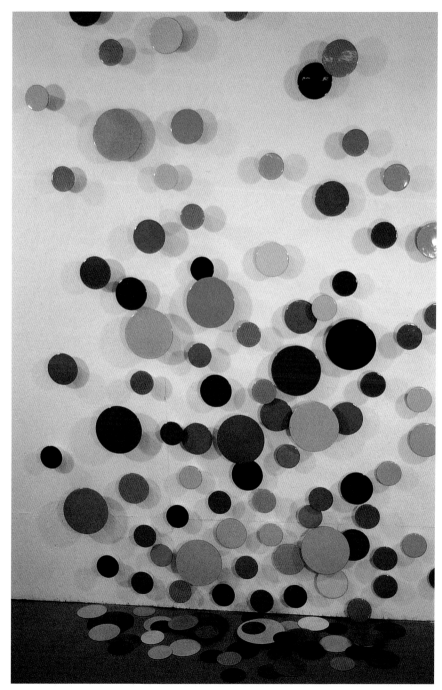

Kate Ward Terry
Party On | 2005
2.7 X 3.4 M
Copper, enamel; sifted, glued

Deborah Lozier
Blue Bedspread (Wall Piece) | 2004
4 X 15.5 X 15.5 CM
Copper, steel, enamel; limoges, wet packed
PHOTOS BY ARTIST

Blue Bedspread *is part of a series based on childhood memories. The series is made up of simple studies that use color and shape to spark recollections. This piece was inspired by the matching chenille bedspreads that were in the room I used to share with my sister.* DEBORAH LOZIER

Judith Haack

Spinning Top with Interchangeable Disc | 2008

4 X 5 CM

Sterling silver, enamel

PHOTO BY ARTIST

Anna Tai

Galaxy | 2007

6.4 X 3.9 X 1 CM

22-karat gold, 18-karat gold,
carnelian, amethyst, enamel; cloisonné

PHOTO BY GEORGE POST

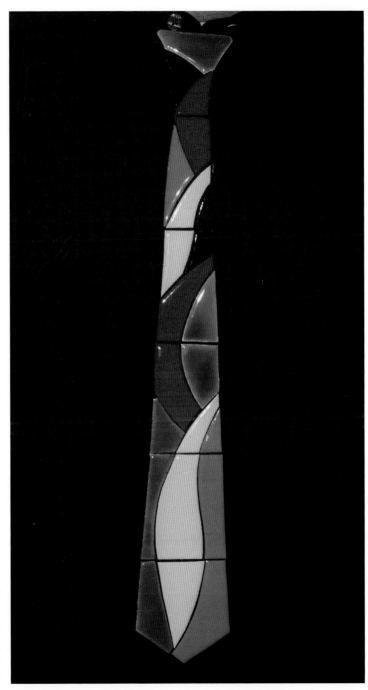

Ingrid I. van der Meer
Stained Glass (Wearable Tie) | 2006
40 X 7 X 0.2 CM
Copper, enamel, felt, hook-and-loop
tape; sifted, kiln fired, glued
PHOTO BY JAN VAN DER MEER

159

Mark Hartung
Untitled | 2007
3 X 5 CM
Copper, enamel; sifted
PHOTO BY ARTIST

John Killmaster
SPEC Center Sculpture | 1976
182.9 X 274.3 X 182.9 CM
Steel, enamel; sprayed,
shaped, stenciled, sgraffito
PHOTOS BY ARTIST

Over the years, I've explored the
possibilities of porcelain enamel, a
medium usually limited to industrial
applications, by developing a synthesis
of traditional techniques, which I call
sgraffito-grisaille. In my studio, I use a
kiln capable of handling up to 22 inches
(55.8 cm) of square and shaped pieces.
This allows me to explore large scale
enameling. JOHN KILLMASTER

161

Kim Lucci-Elbualy

The Spirit (LOVE) | 2005

EACH SIDE, 29 X 96 X 318 CM

Copper, enamel, stainless steel cable, acrylic; die formed, welded, sprayed, kiln fired, sifted, brushed, torch fired, suspended

PHOTOS BY ARTIST

Katy Bergman Cassell

Since Mossadeq was Exiled . . . | 2004

92 X 122 X 1.3 CM

Enamel, copper, handmade ceramic
decals, patching plaster, wood;
stenciled, sifted, image transfer, mounted

PHOTOS BY ARTIST

Ewa Buksa-Klinowska

Water | 2007

7.5 X 9 X 6 CM

Sterling silver, enamel;
plique-à-jour, filigree

PHOTO BY ARTIST

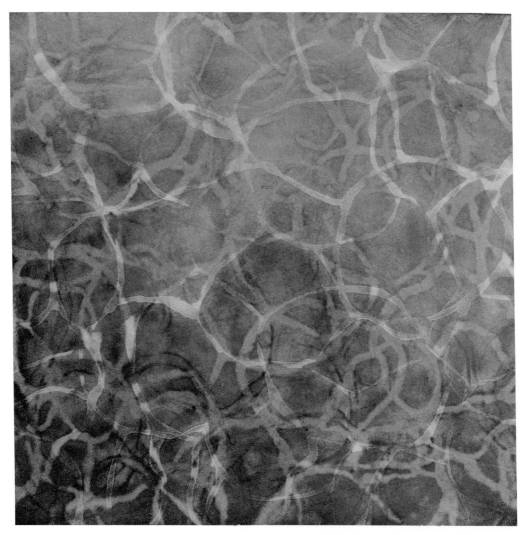

Gretchen Goss
Waterview | 2006
38 X 41 X 1 CM
Enamel, copper; sifted, painted
PHOTO BY ARTIST

Callie Huskins

Tea on the Brain | 2008

10.2 X 3.8 X 1.3 CM

Copper, enamel, paint; sifted,
kiln fired, rivet and tab set

PHOTO BY LINDA DARTY

Melissa Miller

Madeleine | 2008

18 X 17 X 13 CM

Copper, enamel, felt, gilding metal, silver plate, sterling silver; raised, constructed, wet packed, under fired, wet felted

PHOTOS BY ARTIST

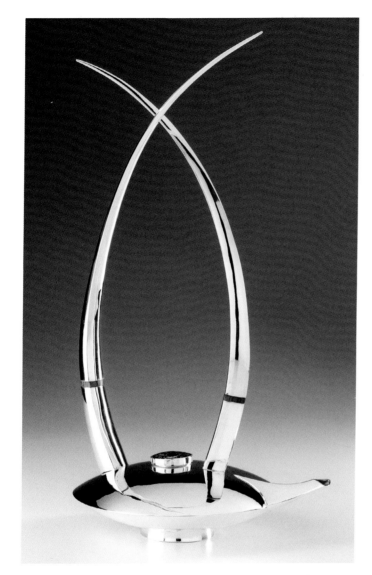

Maureen Banner
Michael Banner
Red Top Teapot | 2007
40.6 X 20.3 X 15.2 CM
Sterling silver, enamel, fine silver; cloisonné, hollow
formed, anticlastic raised, bezel mounted

PHOTOS BY JOHN POLLAK

Tamar De Vries Winter

Three Spice Boxes | 2006

TALLEST, 8 X 5.6 X 5.1 CM

Sterling silver, gold, enamel;
photo etched, hand engraved, riveted

PHOTOS BY PETER MENNIM

Leslie Laine Lewis
From Duckling to Swan | 2008
30 X 41 X 29 CM
Fine silver, copper, enamel, black pearls, patina,
liver of sulfur; woven, pierced, sifted, kiln fired
PHOTOS BY ROBLY A. GLOVER

When I was a little girl, my mother read the story of the ugly duckling to me. She always assured me that one day I'd grow up to be beautiful like the swan in the story. This piece allows the wearer to superficially take on the beauty of the swan. It's adorned with two pierced swans floating among water lilies and composed of hundreds of enameled feathers attached to a weaving of fine silver that represents the beauty of a black swan.

LESLIE LAINE LEWIS

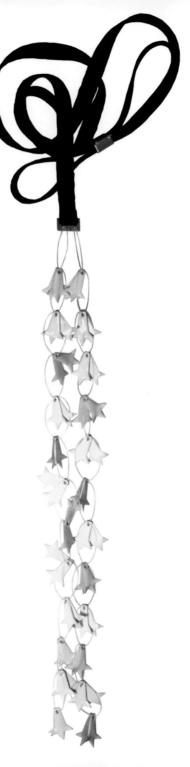

Lonny Fechner
White Spikes Falling from a Black Bent | 2007
60 X 10 X 1 CM
Enamel, fine silver, silver; bent
PHOTO BY ARTIST

I-Ting Wang

Journey | 2003

31 X 5.5 X 5 CM

Copper, enamel; fabricated, wet packed

PHOTO BY KUEN LUNG TSAI

*For me, the potency of enamel
lies in its true nature. Like water,
it's amorphous, composed of moving
molecules that are slowed almost to a
standstill. Working with enamel, you
feel that you can control time, color,
and energy, but it's only an illusion.*

MELISSA MANLEY

Melissa Manley
Cup | 2006
12 X 9 CM
Copper, enamel; raised, chased, sifted
PHOTO BY ARTIST

Patricia Case
Blue Rim Bowls | 2007
LEFT, 5.1 X 7.6 X 7.6; RIGHT, 5.1 X 8.9 X 8.9 CM
Copper, silver, enamel; raised, fabricated
PHOTO BY ARTIST

I-Ting Wang
Still | 2004
33 X 6.5 X 5.5 CM
Copper, enamel, silverplate;
wet packed, die formed
PHOTO BY KUEN LUNG TSAI

Harold B. Helwig

Bed, Sheet, and Pillow Series: Inner Edges | 1990

30.5 X 20.4 X 5 CM

Low-carbon steel, enamel; coated, camaïeu

PHOTO BY MEL MITTERMILLER

Ralph Bakker
Acer Sacharum | 2007
DIAMETER, 20 CM
Gold, silver, enamel; sifted,
kiln fired, assembled
PHOTOS BY ARTIST

*This necklace is strong in form even
though it's made for the sensitive
area between neck and breast, a
transitional place on the body. Stemming
from an ancient tradition, the chain-mail
links make these pieces into objects that
naturally form themselves to the body.*
RALPH BAKKER

Claudia Milić
Untitled | 2008
10.5 X 2.5 X 0.5 CM
Fine silver, enamel; sifted
PHOTO BY TOM NASSAL

Susan Kingsley

The Epiffany Collection | 2002

VARIOUS DIMENSIONS

Felt, sterling silver, fine silver,
enamel; sifted, die formed

PHOTO BY ROBERT NEIMY

 These pieces are about seduction and synthetic love. I made the works during a residency at the Kohler Company, where a wide array of sinks, tubs, and other home products are made and enameled, and so I was given access to the company's colors. I wanted these pieces to reflect an intoxicating display of abundance and manufactured sensuality.

JOHN J. RAIS

John J. Rais
Handbag Grouping | 2006
EACH, 32 X 40 X 30 CM
Iron, brass, enamel; cast, chromeplated
PHOTOS BY KOHLER CO

Minwon Kim

Honey-Plant (Fun to Choose) | 2007

CONTAINER, 7.4 X 7.4 X 6.1 CM
EACH RING, 1.8 X 1.8 X 2.5 CM

Sterling silver, enamel, fine silver, 14-karat gold, cotton cord; torch fired, bezel set, crocheted

PHOTOS BY BECKY MCDONAH

You Ra Kim
Untitled | 2005

BROOCH, 11 X 5.5 X 0.4 CM
EARRINGS, 5.7 X 1.5 X 0.4 CM

Sterling silver, enamel

PHOTO BY PETRA JASCHKE

Sharon Massey
Pieces of Me Brooches | 2006
EACH, 6 X 6 X 1 CM
Steel, enamel, copper, graphite,
gold, hair; sifted, fabricated
PHOTO BY ROBERT DIAMANTE

Jennifer Halvorson
Cocconeis Vanity | 2007
8.9 X 7.6 X 1.9 CM
Thread, copper, enamel; tatted electroformed,
sifted, wet packed, kiln fired, constructed
PHOTO BY ARTIST

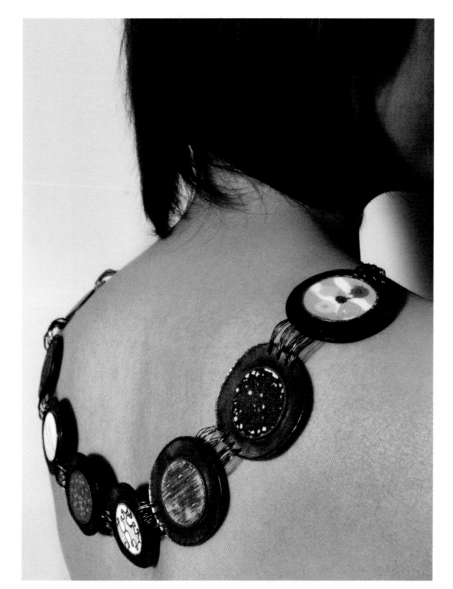

Yung-huei Chao
Day by Day | 2008
EACH, 0.3 X 4.5 X 4.5 CM
Copper, enamel; oxidized, sifted, wet packed,
cloisonné, over fired, under fired
PHOTOS BY ARTIST

Seth Papac
Untitled | 2006

5 X 5 X 3 CM

Sterling silver, fine silver, enamel;
granulated, sifted, under fired, prong set

PHOTO BY MARIA PHILLIPS

Tamar De Vries Winter
Leaf Cup | 2008
75 X 55 CM
Sterling silver, enamel; spun, machine engraved
PHOTO BY PETER MENNIM

Heather Wang
Lace Plique-á-Jour Dish | 2008
7.5 X 7.5 X 1.5 CM
Sterling silver, enamel; plique-à-jour
PHOTOS BY ARTIST

Rebecca Anderson
Under the Veil #2 | 2007
14 X 10 X 8 CM
Copper, enamel, sterling silver;
electroformed, chased, repoussé, sifted
PHOTO BY ARTIST

Patricia Peterson
Garden Vines #1 | 2008
13 X 11 X 1.5 CM
Sterling silver, enamel; cloisonné

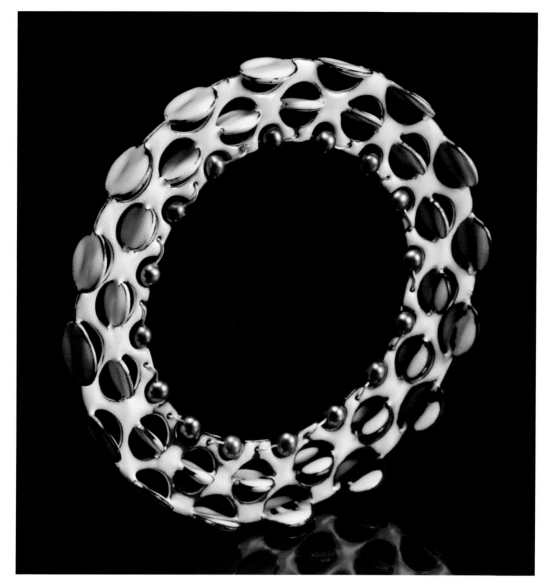

Jim Norton

Black Pearl Bracelet | 2007

9 X 9 X 1 CM

Copper, enamel, pearls;
dipped, kiln fired, wired

PHOTO BY ARTIST

Susie Ganch

Reach | 2007

35 X 35 X 56.3 CM

Steel, copper, enamel; fabricated

PHOTOS BY TAYLOR DABNEY

Aran Galligan
Truffle Bowl | 2007
10 X 20 X 20 CM
Steel, enamel; forged, pierced, fabricated
PHOTO BY STEVE MANN

Kirsten Haydon
Ice Funnel, Ice Melts
(Object and Earrings) | *2007*

OBJECT, 8 X 6 X 4 CM
LARGEST EARRING, 4 X 2.3 X 1 CM

Copper, steel, enamel, reflector beads;
spun, soldered, sifted, painted, kiln fired

PHOTO BY JEREMY DILLON

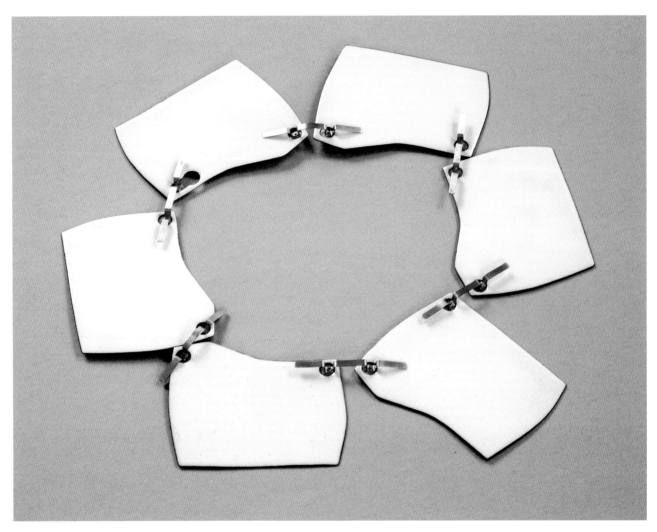

Beate Eismann
Alas Blancas | 2003
LENGTH, 10 CM
Copper, enamel, gold; sawed, riveted
PHOTO BY ARTIST

Sarah Abramson
Volume I | 2007
9 X 8 X 6 CM
Copper, sterling silver, silk thread, enamel;
electroformed, fabricated, sifted, sewn

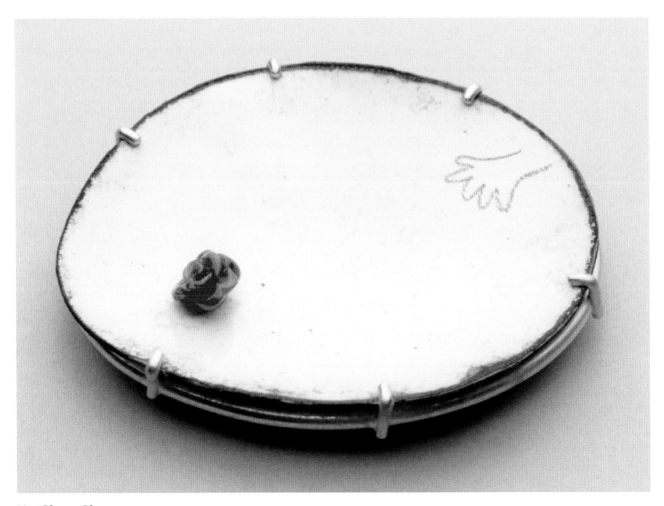

Yu-Chun Chen

Untitled | 2004

4 X 5 X 0.6 CM

Copper, enamel, silver, coral; sifted, prong set

PHOTO BY FEDERICO CAVICCHIOLI

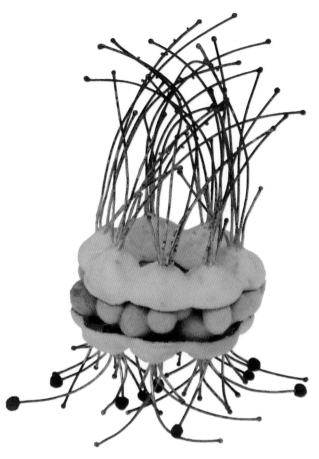

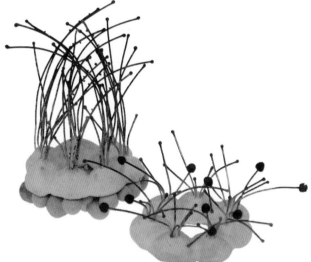

Melissa Miller
Object Reminiscent of Things Past, No. 4 | 2007
15 X 9 X 11 CM
Copper, enamel, sterling silver, fine silver, felt;
repoussé, granulated, sifted, under fired, wet felted
PHOTOS BY ARTIST

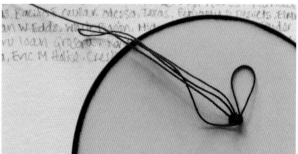

Helen Carnac

Lost | 2007

25 X 25 X 2 CM

Enamel, white board, thread, plywood, steel, paper, pencil

Roberta Bernabei Shaw
Trasformazione #2
(Brooch) | 2006
1 X 8 X 40 CM
Sterling silver, foam,
cotton, enamel; laser cut,
cast, oxidized
PHOTO BY ALAN DUNCAN

Dubbelop
Snow White, Bracelet | 2004
8 X 10 X 1 CM
Titanium, enamel; kiln fired
PHOTO BY JAN MATTESIUS

Sarah Abramson
Grid | 2007
12 X 8 X 3 CM
Copper, sterling silver, enamel;
electroformed, fabricated, hydraulically
formed, sifted, prong set
PHOTO BY JAMES FOSSETT

Liz Steiner
Rock Necklace | 2007
60 X 8 X 8 CM
Copper, enamel, thread; electroformed,
sifted, kiln fired, knitted
PHOTO BY ARTIST

René Roberts
Tafoni Formation No. 1 | 2005
30 X 45 X 1.5 CM

Copper, enamel, glass stainers'
colors; photoetched, sifted, wet packed,
painted, basse taille, wall mounted

PHOTO BY ARTIST

Meagan Clark
Untitled | 2008
14 X 7 X 2 CM
Fine silver, copper, liquid enamel; wire wrapped
PHOTO BY LINDA DARTY

Valerie Mitchell
Tri-Nodule Pendant | 2000
11 X 3 CM
Copper, enamel, sterling silver;
hollow formed, electroformed, kiln fired,
sifted, hand constructed, oxidized
PHOTO BY MARK JOHANN

In my work I try to capture a sense of impermanence, a fleeting moment in a continuum of transformation. The forms that structure the pieces represent not only what is seen but also what is not. I envision the pieces as containers, yet what they hold is a mystery, like a seed that hasn't yet revealed its secrets. The enamel acts as a shell, both fragile and protective. It contains and defines the interior space. SUSAN REMNANT

Susan Remnant

Enigma | 2004

14 X 3.5 X 1.5 CM

Sterling silver, copper, enamel, fine silver; cloisonné, sifted, cast, constructed

PHOTO BY ARTIST

Kristina Glick Shank
Shells and Spirals | 2007
LENGTH, 46 CM
Enamel, found objects, pearls, sterling silver,
copper, patina; sifted, painted, electroformed
PHOTOS BY ARTIST

Lisa Crowder

Bunnies Light and Dark; Two Brooches | 2007

EACH, 8 X 3 X 0.7 CM

Sterling silver, copper, enamel; sifted, torch fired,
tab set, etched, oxidized, hydraulic die formed

PHOTO BY HAP SAKWA

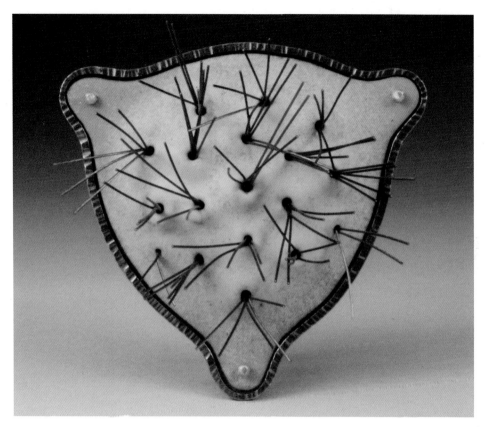

Danielle Embry
Pincushion 1.5: Mammalaria ashieldformis | 2005
6 X 6 X 3.5 CM
Sterling silver, enamel, copper, beading
wire; chased, cold connected
PHOTO BY ARTIST

Amanda Bristow

Arctic Adventure Set | 2007

BOX, 8 X 15 X 15 CM
ANIMALS, 5–9 CM

Copper, enamel, graphite, fabric,
cardboard, acrylic paint, floral foam;
electroformed, sifted

PHOTOS BY ARTIST

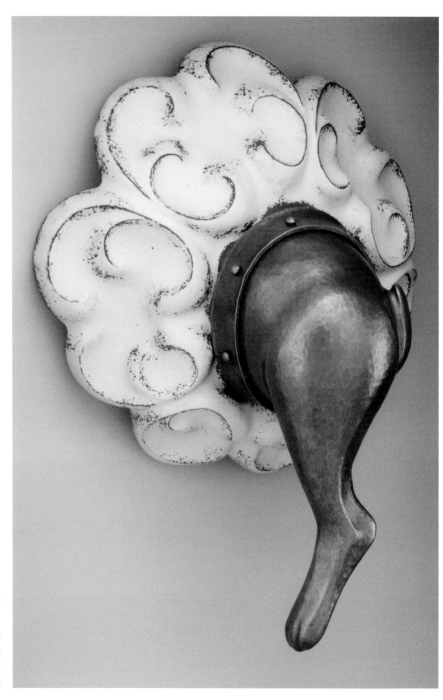

Miel-Margarita Paredes
Bound | 2005

38 X 25 X 15 CM

Copper, enamel, brass, patina;
raised, chased, welded, sifted

PHOTO BY STEPHEN FUNK

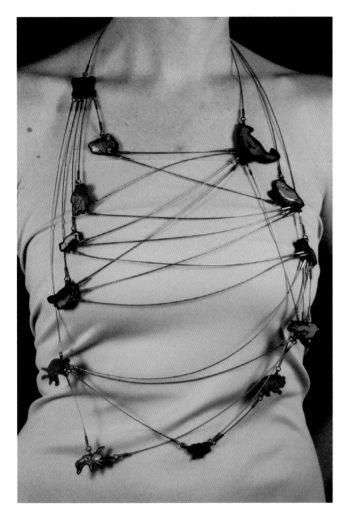

Tanesa Flavell
Food Web Necklace | 2008
LENGTH, 118 CM
Copper, sterling silver, stainless steel
cable, enamel; champlevé
PHOTOS BY JESSICA SCHLACHTER-TOWNSEND

My work investigates the fine line between our fascination with and disgust of insects, the most diverse group of organisms on the planet. Even a lowly mosquito can be admired for its adornment of tiny, intricate hairs, complex transparent wing patterns, and incredible life history. One viewer might cringe, while another might smile. CHARITY L. HALL

Charity L. Hall
Crabs: Papillon d'Amour (Belt Buckle) | 2007
7 X 9 X 1 CM
Copper, silver, enamel, garnet; sgraffito
PHOTO BY ARTIST

Michael Romanik

White-Breasted Nuthatch (Brooch) | 2006

5.2 X 5.2 X 1 CM

Enamel, fine silver, sterling silver, 18-karat gold,
22-karat gold, 24-karat gold, iolite; cloisonné,
roller textured, stamped, etched, bezel set

PHOTO BY LARRY SANDERS

Michele Raney
Raven | 2007
3 X 5 CM
Fine silver, 24-karat gold, enamel;
hand carved, die struck
PHOTO BY RALPH GABRINER

Kathleen Wilcox

Floridance Quilt: Egret | 2006

25 X 25 X 1 CM

Copper, enamel, gold, silver foil, copper
wire; sifted, screen-printed, inlaid,
overglazed, kiln fired, assembled, glued

PHOTOS BY RICHARD BRUNCK

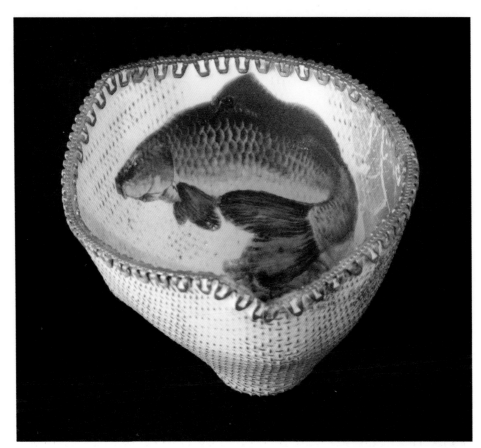

June Jasen
Yellow-Bellied Palm Vessel | 2006–2007
8 X 10 CM
Enamel, copper cloth; fused
PHOTO BY ARTIST

Tedd R. McDonah

Petal Limited | 2005

EACH, 7.6 X 2.5 X 1.3 CM

Copper, enamel, galvanized
steel; sifted, kiln fired

PHOTO BY ARTIST

Marilena Ramenzoni
Ramenzoni-Globo | 2006
17 X 17 CM
Copper, enamel, silver
PHOTO BY ARTIST

Anna Moll
Fish | 2007

8 X 5 X 1.5 CM

Sterling silver, enamel, glass, pearls, steel wire

PHOTO BY GEORGE MEISTER

Mary Klein
Fish #1 | 2007

35 X 15 X 5 CM

Copper, enamel, silestone material; cut, sawed, sifted, painted, mounted, engraved

PHOTO BY ARTIST

Nancy Sickbert-Wheeler
Untitled | 2006
6 X 4 X 0.1 CM
Copper, enamel; etched, champlevé
PHOTO BY RALPH GABRINER

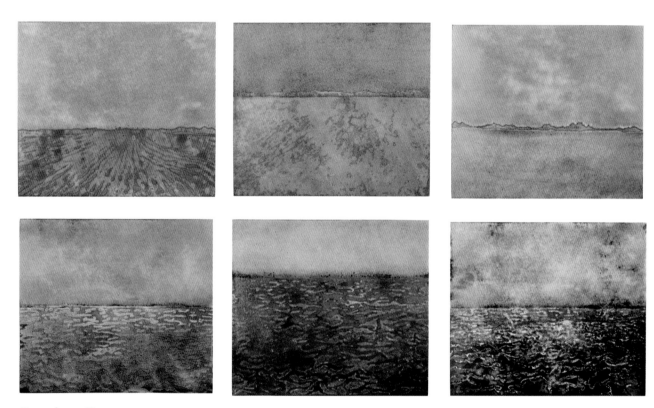

Gretchen Goss

Wayne County and South Manitou | 2007

34 X 58 X 1 CM

Enamel, copper; sifted

PHOTO BY ARTIST

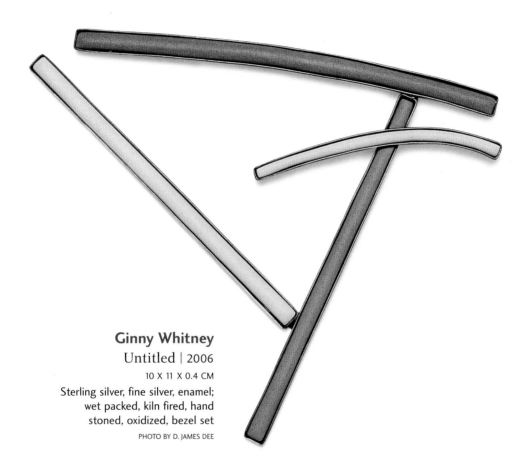

Ginny Whitney
Untitled | 2006
10 X 11 X 0.4 CM
Sterling silver, fine silver, enamel;
wet packed, kiln fired, hand
stoned, oxidized, bezel set
PHOTO BY D. JAMES DEE

Melissa Huff
Two-Headed Lily | 2001
10 X 4 X 3 CM
Copper, enamel; electroformed,
wet packed, kiln fired
PHOTO BY WILMER ZEHR

Stephanie Tomczak
Xenophora | 2005
6.4 X 6.6 X 2.3 CM
Copper, enamel, silver; bonded, under fired
PHOTO BY ARTIST

Pamela Moore

Natural Elements | 2007

50.8 X 457.2 X 5.1 CM

Copper, pipe, enamel, hand-tinted
glass; engraved, drilled, kiln fired,
soldered, wired

PHOTOS BY ARTIST

Deborah Lozier
Balancing Act | 2005
20 X 17.2 X 14 CM
Copper, steel, enamel;
limoges, sifted
PHOTOS BY ARTIST

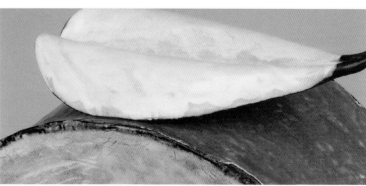

Kathryn Osgood

Pink Pierced Ocean Flower | 2007

7 X 7 X 1.5 CM

Sterling silver, copper, fine silver,
enamel, pearls; fabricated, sifted

PHOTO BY ROBERT DIAMANTE

Barbi Gossen
Rosa Autoeroticus | 2008
7 X 20 X 17 CM
Fine silver, copper, enamel; formed,
chased, welded, sifted, wet packed
PHOTO BY ARTIST

Sofia Björkman
Brooch | 2006
6 X 4 X 2 CM
Silver, enamel; burned, cast
PHOTO BY ARTIST

John McVeigh
Lichen III, Brooch | 2007
5.9 X 3.5 X 0.9 CM
Sterling silver, copper, liquid enamel; pierced,
formed, torch fired, sifted, etched, riveted
PHOTO BY ROBERT DIAMANTE

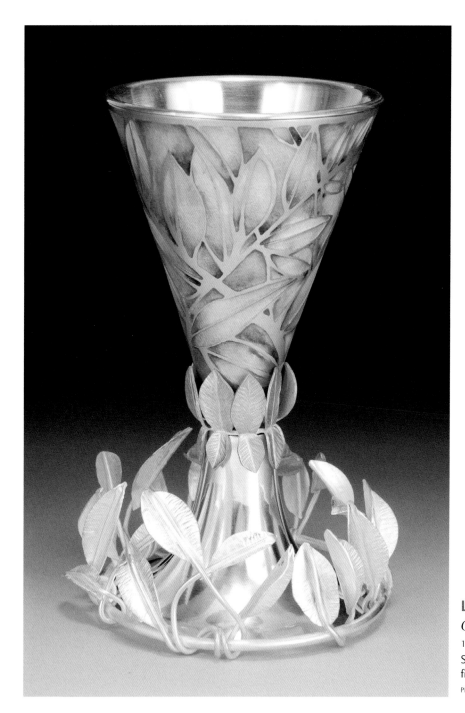

Linda Darty
Outside In: Branches | 2007
15.2 X 8.9 X 8.9 CM
Sterling silver, enamel,
fine silver; champlevé
PHOTO BY ARTIST

Bokhee Jung

The Sweet Seventeen | 2006

LARGEST, 17 X 14 CM

Fine silver, silver,
enamel, lapis lazuli

PHOTO BY IN-KYU OH

Harlan W. Butt
Earth Beneath Our Feet:
Texas Horizon #4 | 2007

12 X 15 X 15 CM

Fine silver, enamel, sterling silver,
14-karat gold; cloisonné, limoges

PHOTO BY RAFAEL MOLINA

Maria Papalia
Forest Reliquaries | 2007
26 X 51 X 51 CM
Paper, clay, thread, wax, copper,
enamel; sifted, kiln fired
PHOTO BY ARTIST

Yeonmi Kang

Breath | 2003

5.5 X 4.8 X 2 CM

Sterling silver, enamel, 24-karat
gold; kum boo, cast, kiln fired

PHOTO BY ARTIST

David C. Freda

Green Slipper Brooch | 2006

12.7 X 5.1 X 3.8 CM

24-karat yellow gold, 20-karat yellow gold,
18-karat yellow gold, tanzanite, diamonds, enamel;
cast, fabricated, granulated, prong set

PHOTO BY DAVID BEHL

Angela Gerhard
Necklace for Spring | 2008
43.2 X 10.8 CM
Sterling silver, 18-karat gold, copper, enamel; sifted, etched, soldered
PHOTO BY ROBERT DIAMANTE

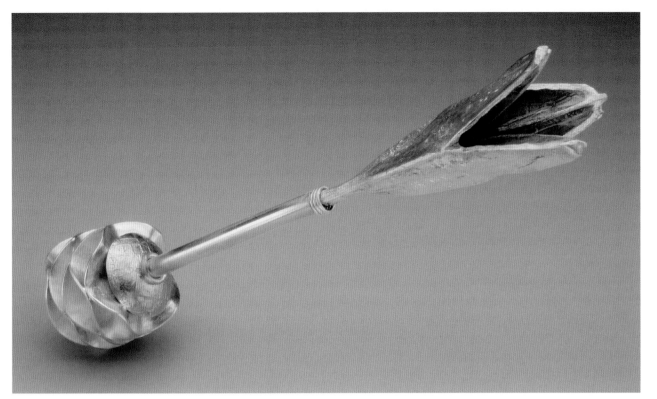

Gail Nelson

Honey Dipper | 2007

12.7 X 2.4 X 2.4 CM

Sterling silver, enamel, 24-karat gold;
kum boo, soldered, tessellated, cast

PHOTO BY BILL LEMKE

Leia Zumbro
Triform | 2007
8.5 X 11.5 X 6 CM
Copper, enamel; raised, chased,
sifted, kiln fired, etched
PHOTO BY BLAKE LARUE

Kate Cathey
White Layered Cups | 2004
EACH, 7.7 X 6.4 X 6.4 CM
Copper, enamel; formed, chased, tabbed,
sifted, painted, stenciled, over fired
PHOTO BY ROBERT DIAMANTE

Sarah Perkins
Cactus Container III | 2006
16.5 X 12.7 X 12.7 CM
Fine silver, enamel, tourmaline; fabricated

Dorothy Barrett

In the Midst of the Incomprehensible #4 | 1999

3.3 X 8.3 X 1.3 CM

Fine silver, sterling silver, enamel; etched, basse taille

PHOTOS BY JASON S.K. TAN

This piece was inspired by my experiences as an American living in Japan. I found myself alternately fascinated and frustrated by the contrasts that exist between two dramatically different cultures. Communication between cultures, I discovered, can't be achieved solely through translation of language. We must learn to read between the cultural lines. DOROTHY BARRETT

As a trained architect, I'm interested in the interplay of surface, volume, and space. I treat the copper substrate of enameling not only as a support for images but as a medium in its own right. It can be shaped, sewn, etched, folded, or bent to create a volume that synergizes with the enamel's color, texture, and sheen. Whether a sculptural object or jewelry, my pieces explore metal and enamel as equals. MARSHA K. POWELL

Marsha K. Powell
Wheelie | 2006
21.6 X 12.7 X 9.5 CM
Copper, gold, enamel, found wheels; punched, sewn, sifted, brushed, kiln fired, mounted
PHOTO BY D. JAMES DEE

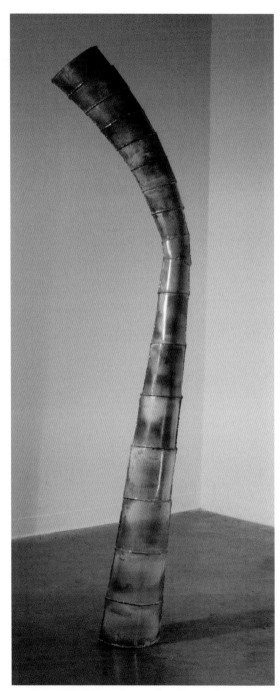

Jessica Schlachter-Townsend
Form Through Fire: 122707 | 2007
226 X 25.4 X 61 CM
Copper, enamel; sprayed, brushed,
torch fired, oxyacetylene welded
PHOTOS BY ARTIST

Averill B. Shepps
Purple Bowl with Trees | 2004
24 X 12.5 CM
Copper, fine silver, enamel; sifted, rolled
PHOTO BY JERRY ANTHONY

My childhood was spent on the North Atlantic, in Ireland, where the landscape was composed of ancient rocks and wild seas. I now live in central London and try to make sense of my early experiences. My work deals with fragments of memory overlaid with the patina of time. JOAN MACKARELL

Joan MacKarell
Archives in the Peat; Badges | 2007
11 X 2 X 1 CM
Copper, enamel, sand, terra cotta; sifted
PHOTO BY PENNY DAVIS

Soyeon Kim
Object 01 | 2008
10 X 9 X 5 CM
Copper, enamel; electroformed, sifted
PHOTO BY ARTIST

Mark Hartung
Untitled | 2006
20 X 36 X 36 CM
Copper, enamel; sifted
PHOTO BY ARTIST

Mirjam Hiller
Brooch | 2007
4 X 8 X 6 CM
Copper, sterling silver, enamel; rough fired
PHOTOS BY PETRA JASCHKE

Beate Klockmann
Spoon | 2002
17 X 3 X 2 CM
Enamel, silver, gold;
hammered, fabricated
PHOTOS BY ARTIST

Tania Carson
Be Mine | 2005

11 X 16.5 X 7.5 CM

Recycled steel can, found cupboard
handles, enamel; kiln fired

PHOTO BY JAMES CHAMPION

Jean Tudor

My Life/Her Life: Aurora | 2000

27 X 32.5 X 2.5 CM

Copper, enamel, silver, decal, Ecuadorian
grave doll; wet inlay, cloisonné

PHOTO BY ARTIST

253

Greg Flint
Digital Muse #7 | 2005
10 X 10 CM
Enamel, steel, photo transfer; wet packed
PHOTO BY ARTIST

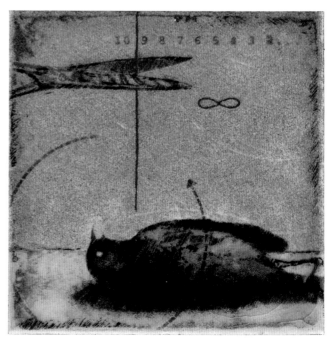

Greg Flint
Ellegy | 2006
10 X 10 CM
Enamel, steel, photo transfer;
wet packed, painted
PHOTO BY ARTIST

Ora Kuller
A Safe Haven in the Storm | 2004–2008

63.5 X 45.7 X 3.5 CM

Enamel, oxides, watercolors, fine silver, sterling silver, copper, brass, sterling silver, 24-karat gold; sifted, wet packed, etched, bezel set, fabricated, cloisonné, plique-à-jour

PHOTOS BY GIORA K. KULLER

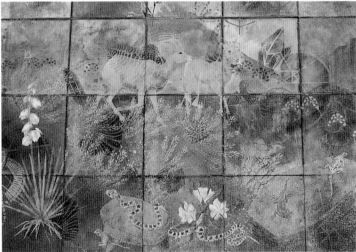

Patricia R. Musick

Infinite Nature | 1998

3.12 X 7 M

Copper, silver foil, enamel; sifted, painted, sgraffito, mounted

PHOTOS BY ARTIST

Nancy Mellody Bentley
Forbidden Places: Morning, Noon, and Night | 2004

BROOCHES, 8.9 X 2.7 CM
BOXES, 19.7 X 24.8 CM

Sterling silver, brass, enamel, board, graphite,
colored pencil; sifted, bezel set, painted

PHOTO BY ARTIST

Juanita Lee Hill

Bed of Life | 2005

19.5 X 10.5 X 20.5 CM

Enamel, agate, bronze, brass, bolts, nuts;
soldered, sifted, painted, cast, bezel set

PHOTO BY KAREN CARTER

Helen Aitken-Kuhnen
Egg Cups | 2000
EACH, 2.2 X 9 X 9 CM
Sterling silver, enamel; spun
PHOTO BY JOHANNES KUHNEN

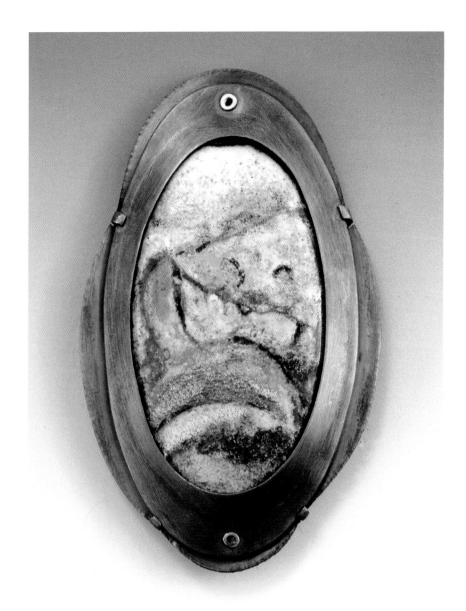

Callie Huskins
Still Life of Cheese and Limes | 2008
10.2 X 3.8 X 1.3 CM
Copper, enamel, paint; sifted, kiln fired, rivet and tab set
PHOTO BY LINDA DARTY

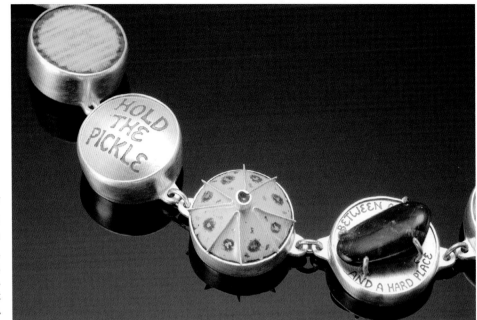

Carol Salisbury

Pickle Necklace | 2006

1.3 X 45 X 2 CM

Sterling silver, copper, enamel, gold, stone, acrylic, watercolor, paper, polymer clay; cloisonné, fabricated, bezel set

PHOTOS BY DAN KUITKA

Jutta Klingebiel
Ein Paar Wiener | 2003
DIAMETER, 1.6 CM
18-karat gold, enamel; painted
PHOTO BY ARTIST

Jutta Klingebiel
Nest | 2008
4.5 X 4.5 X 1 CM
Sterling silver, enamel; painted
PHOTO BY CHRISTIAN CHIRULESCU

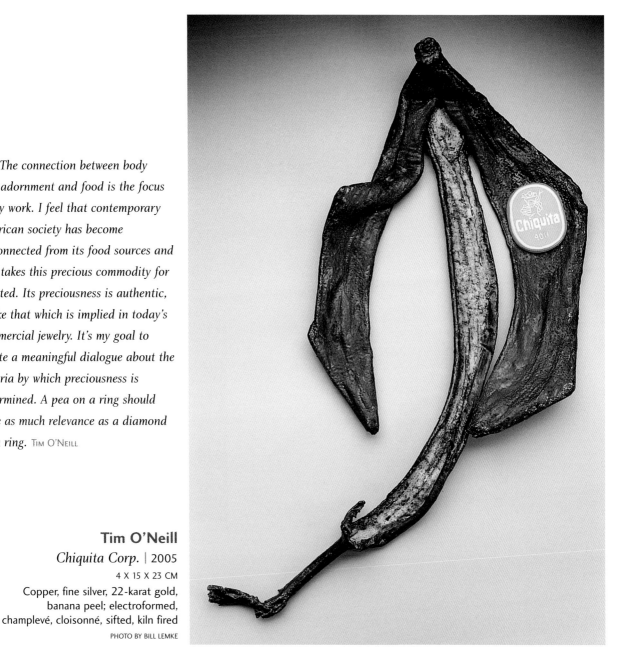

The connection between body adornment and food is the focus of my work. I feel that contemporary American society has become disconnected from its food sources and now takes this precious commodity for granted. Its preciousness is authentic, unlike that which is implied in today's commercial jewelry. It's my goal to create a meaningful dialogue about the criteria by which preciousness is determined. A pea on a ring should have as much relevance as a diamond on a ring. TIM O'NEILL

Tim O'Neill
Chiquita Corp. | 2005
4 X 15 X 23 CM
Copper, fine silver, 22-karat gold, banana peel; electroformed, champlevé, cloisonné, sifted, kiln fired
PHOTO BY BILL LEMKE

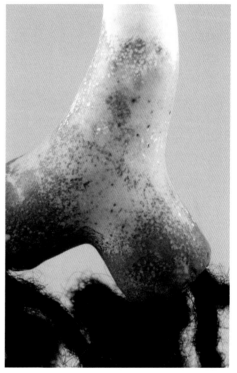

Ruth Zelanski

Synaptic Pendant (III) | 2006

15 X 9 X 2 CM

Copper, enamel, sterling silver, wool, steel
cable; electroformed, sifted, sandblasted,
crocheted, fulled, needle felted, fabricated

PHOTOS BY ARTIST

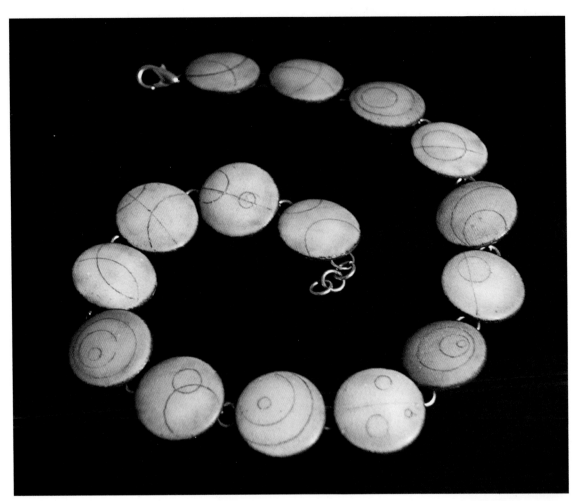

Kimberly Geiser
Untitled Necklace | 2006
3 X 60 X 0.5 CM
Copper, sterling silver, enamel;
sifted, kiln fired, matte finish
PHOTO BY ARTIST

Giovanni Sicuro (Minto)

M1 | 2007

4.7 X 7 CM

Silver, enamel; hollow constructed

PHOTO BY LAURA TESSARO

Shava Lena Lawson
*Sounds of the Season
Series: Spring* | 2001
21.6 X 13.3 X 0.6 CM
Sterling silver, fine silver,
enamel; sifted, blanked
PHOTO BY DOUG YAPLE

Mark Kummeth
Plique-à-Jour #2 | 2006
6 X 14 CM
Fine silver, enamel; plique-à-jour, etched

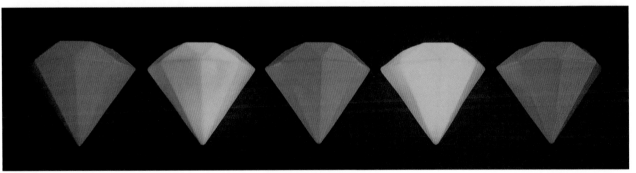

Veleta Vancza
Carbonado Series | 2006
EACH, 45.7 X 40.6 X 30.5 CM
Cast iron, phosphorescent enamel; sifted
PHOTOS BY KOHLER CO.

Jo Lu

Bracelet | 2004

9 X 8 X 8 CM

Copper, enamel; sifted, riveted

Kirsten Haydon
Ice Airfield (Brooch) | 2007
12.2 X 7.8 X 1.5 CM
Copper, silver, steel, enamel, reflector beads; oxidized,
fabricated, extended firing, photo transfer
PHOTO BY JEREMY DILLON

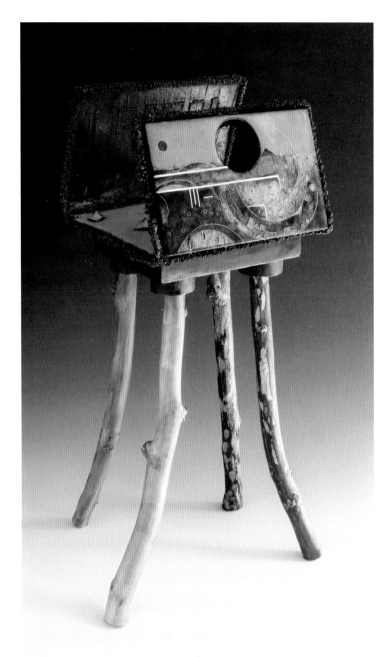

My process is one of forging forward, stepping back, designing and redesigning, constructing and deconstructing, thinking and rethinking. I realize the connection between my conscious aesthetic and subconscious references to my personal history and continuing journey. It's my hope that viewers will discover their own personal references in my work and layer those references upon mine, thus allowing the work to exist in many incarnations.

ABBY SCHINDLER GOLDBLATT

Abby Schindler Goldblatt
Primordial | 2008
41.5 X 23 X 18 CM

Copper, enamel, gold, fine silver, wood, epoxy paste; cloisonné, electroformed, constructed

PHOTOS BY PAMELA ZILLY

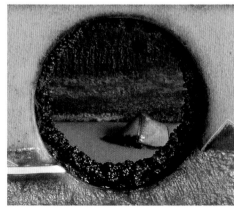

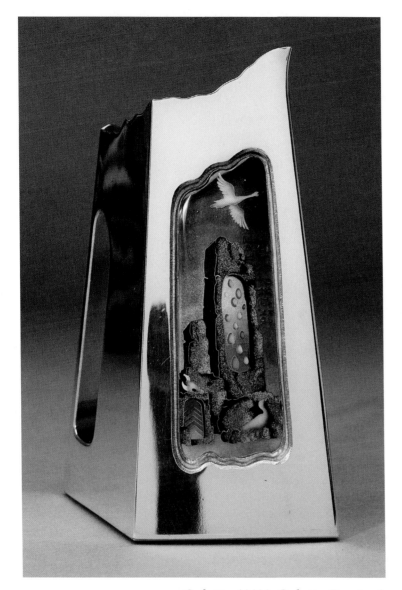

Colette (AKA Colette Denton)

Water Pitcher #2 | 1983

20.3 X 15.9 X 7.6 CM

Sterling silver, fine silver, 24-karat gold, 22-karat
gold; cloisonné, painted, bezel set, fabricated

PHOTOS BY ARTIST

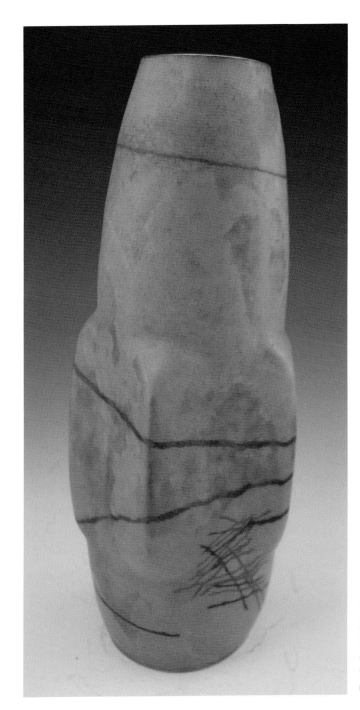

Sarah Perkins
Stepping Formation | 2008
22.8 X 12.7 X 11.4 CM
Copper, enamel;
welded, fabricated
PHOTO BY ARTIST

Ingeborg Vandamme
Diary Necklace | 1995
DIAMETER, 25 CM
Copper, enamel, graphite, paper, thread;
hand fabricated, soldered, formed
PHOTO BY HENNI VAN BEEK

Lisa Crowder

Orange and Black Spiral Double Ring | 2008

2 X 5.7 X 3 CM

Sterling silver, copper, enamel; sifted, torch fired,
fabricated, tab set, oxidized, hydraulic die formed

PHOTO BY HAP SAKWA

Cinelli & Maillet
Collar | 2007
21 X 17 CM
Sterling silver, enamel;
oxidized, kiln fired, riveted
PHOTO BY DONOVAN DAVIS

Marcela M. McLean

Time Cycles | 2006

8.5 X 2.5 CM

Sterling silver, copper, enamel, metal oxides, cubic zirconia; hand painted

PHOTO BY JACK ZILKER

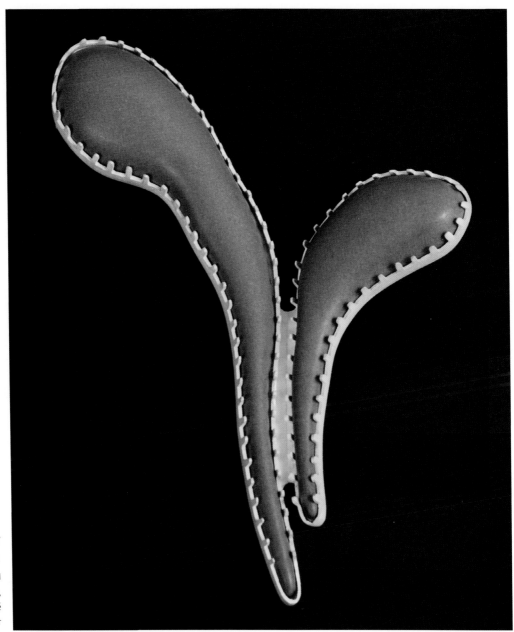

Lynn Batchelder
Body Form I | 2008
9 X 6.5 X 1 CM
Sterling silver, copper,
enamel; repoussé
PHOTO BY ARTIST

Suzanne Kustner
Snail 1 and 2 | 2000
EACH, 5 X 5 X 1 CM
Copper, enamel, gold; sifted, bezel set
PHOTO BY HAP SAKWA

Ellen Goldman
Unfinished Tale | 2005
10 X 3 CM
Sterling silver, enamel, copper;
fired, separated, set
PHOTO BY JHOEKO

G. McLarty

Postcard—The Girls | 2002

13.8 X 8.8 X 0.3 CM

Copper, enamel, assembled images, mica, stamp, brass screws; sifted, champlevé

PHOTOS BY JACK ZILKER

Kathy Aspinall
Neckpiece | 2003
20 X 20 X 0.2 CM
Fine silver, enamel, silkscreen print
PHOTOS BY MEI SEE LIANG-JACKSON

Anita Van Doorn
Rock Pools Series 1 | 2006
4.2 X 3.7 X 3.7 CM
Fine silver, enamel; cast, constructed
PHOTO BY KIRSTEN HAYDON

Yi Chen
Sea Creature #1 | 2008
8 X 12 X 12 CM
Copper, enamel; torch fired, raised
PHOTOS BY ARTIST

Debbie Wetmore

Shaman's Rattle | 2005–2006

30 X 10 X 10 CM

Copper, enamel, silver, horn, hair,
antique glass eye; sifted

PHOTO BY JACK ZILKER

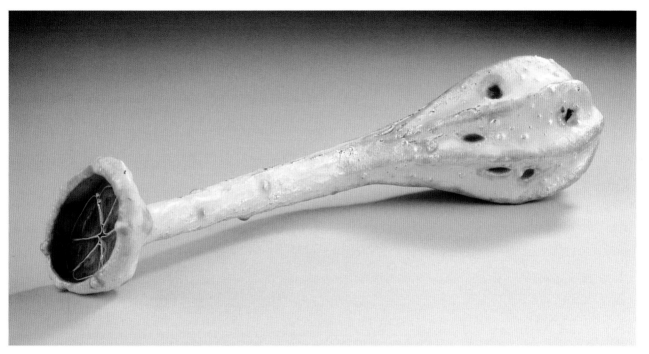

We see our environment every day yet rarely understand it in moments of silent concentration. I'm interested in the moment when we pause to really look at something, try to understand it, and connect to it in some way. In my work I create references to the triggers and mechanisms of this process of examination and awareness. DIANNE REILLY

Dianne Reilly
Form #6 | 2003
23 X 7 X 7 CM
Fine silver, enamel; sifted, wet packed, plique-à-jour, prong set, electroformed
PHOTO BY ARTIST

Erin B. Gray

Denier | 2003

EACH, 5 X 6 X 6 CM

Sterling silver, copper, enamel, gourds,
mustard seed; cloisonné, bezel set

PHOTO BY TIM BARNWELL

Kristi Kloss

Cotton Ball Totem and
Pollen Petal Totem | 2001

TALLEST, 27 X 11 X 2 CM

Copper, enamel, wood, steel,
wool, cotton, hemp, pollen, pod;
electroformed, sifted, kiln fired,
wrapped, machine carved,
painted, felted, bound

PHOTO BY ARTIST

Melissa Huff
Iris Rising | 2001
12 X 3 X 2 CM
Copper, enamel; electroformed,
wet packed, kiln fired
PHOTO BY WILMER ZEHR

Susan McMurray
Hurricane Vessel | 2007
8 X 6 X 6 CM
Sterling silver, enamel; fabricated
PHOTO BY ARTIST

Carly Wright
Untitled | 2004

4.5 X 5.5 X 1 CM

Sterling silver, enamel, fine silver, gold;
champlevé, oxidized, constructed

PHOTO BY ROBERT DIAMANTE

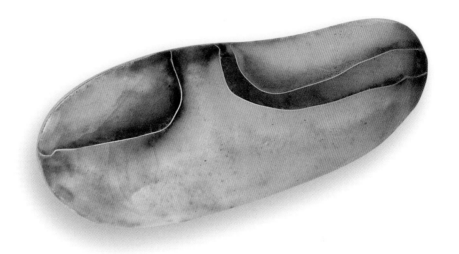

Glenice Lesley Matthews
Memory Rock #3 Walpole | 2006
2.7 X 6.8 X 1 CM
Enamel, fine silver, oxides; cloisonné,
hollow constructed, raised, fabricated
PHOTO BY ARTIST

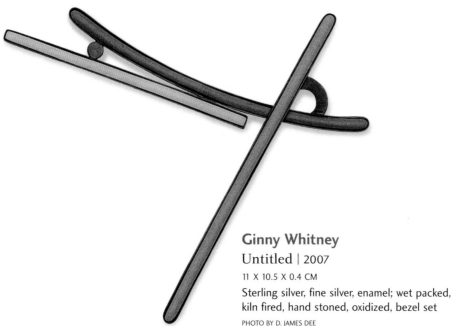

Ginny Whitney
Untitled | 2007
11 X 10.5 X 0.4 CM
Sterling silver, fine silver, enamel; wet packed,
kiln fired, hand stoned, oxidized, bezel set
PHOTO BY D. JAMES DEE

Harold B. Helwig

The Lady Ruth Celadon Series: Float . . . Feelings . . . | 1982

24.9 X 5 CM

Copper; cut, hand engraved, limoges, basse taille, camaïeu

PHOTO BY MEL MITTERMILLER

Mary McBride
Untitled | 2006
5 X 3 X 1.5 CM

Sterling silver, enamel, druzy, glass bullet;
sifted, hand applied, kiln fired, bezel set

Glenice Lesley Matthews
Faggots (Bundles of Sticks) VIII100 | 2007
16 X 1.5 X 1 CM

18-karat yellow gold, 9-karat yellow
gold, sterling silver, enamel; fabricated

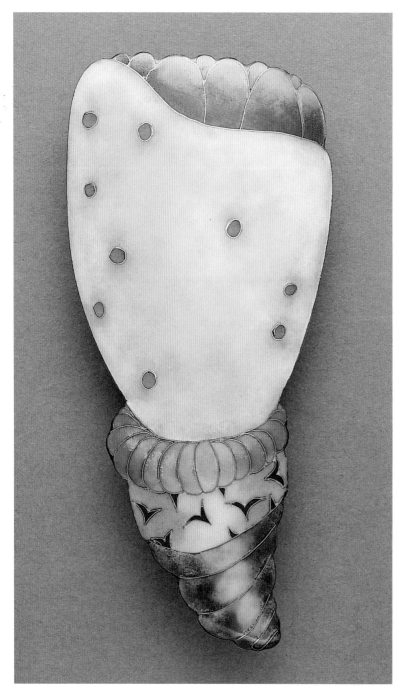

Anne Clark
Untitled | 2000
7.9 X 3.7 X 0.5 CM
Enamel, copper; cloisonné, finished
PHOTO BY ROBERT ELBERT

Martha Banyas
All We Are and All We Seem | 1983
66 X 101.6 X 12.7 CM
Copper, enamel, brass, wood
PHOTO BY ARTIST

Teresa Speer
Churchyard | 2008
6.8 X 4.5 CM
Fine silver, sterling silver, enamel
PHOTO BY ARTIST

Kim Rawdin
The Blue Hotel | 2002
50.8 X 30.5 X 30.5 CM
Copper, enamel, acrylic panel; torch fired
PHOTO BY ARTIST

Yoko Noguchi

I Need a Job | 2008

8.5 X 4 X 16 CM

Aluminum, sterling silver, brass, plastic, rubber,
found object, nuts, bolts, enamel; folded, tap and
die, machine milled, sifted, kiln fired

PHOTO BY ARTIST

Annette Dam
Family Album, 2GB | 2007
35 X 4 X 1.4 CM
Sterling silver, enamel, gold, elastic, felt, 2GB memory stick; transfer
PHOTOS BY ARTIST

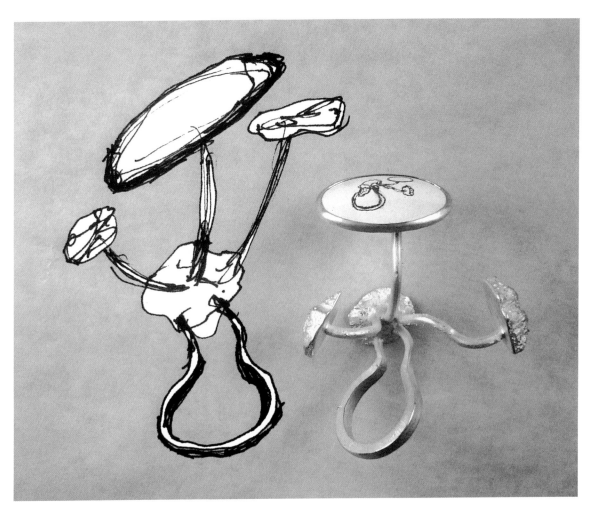

Gabriel Craig
Narcissist No. 6 | 2008
5 X 5 X 6.5 CM
Silver, enamel, graphite; cast, fabricated
PHOTO BY ARTIST

Ashley N. Pierce
Private Thought #1 | 2008
26 X 3.5 CM
Commercial steel
enamelware; sgraffito
PHOTO BY LINDA DARTY

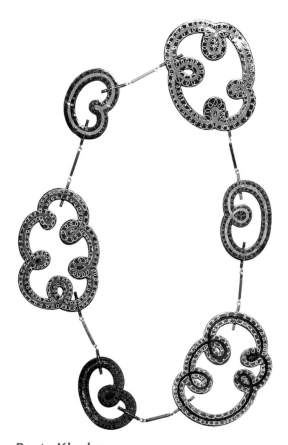

Beate Klockmann
Untitled | 2008
40 X 30 X 0.5 CM
Enamel copper, iron,
gold; fabricated
PHOTO BY ARTIST

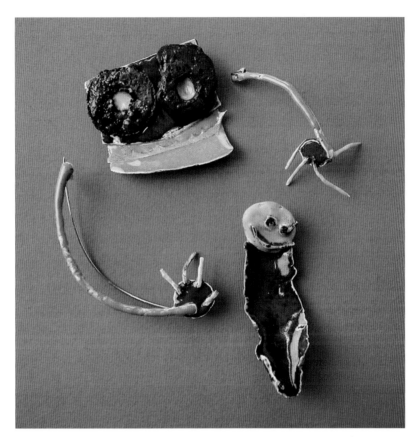

Teresa Lane
Freaks in Love (4-X Brooches) | 2005–2006
3.5 X 6 CM
Fine silver, sterling silver, steel,
gold, enamel; soldered, kiln fired
PHOTO BY ARTIST

Julia Turner
Red Change Brooch | 2007
7 X 5.5 X 1 CM
Sterling silver, enamel, acrylic; under fired
PHOTO BY ARTIST

Nisa Blackmon
Viewing Device No. 1 | 2007
28 X 14 X 17 CM
Copper, enamel; tab constructed,
painted, sifted, kiln fired, assembled
PHOTOS BY ARTIST

307

Joseph Handy

Tube Blanket Brooch | 2006

1.7 X 5.1 X 5.1 CM

Copper, sterling silver, terry cloth,
enamel; formed, fabricated

PHOTO BY ARTIST

Elizabeth Kaprow
Red Cross Brooch | 2007
4.2 X 3.7 X 0.2 CM
Copper, sterling silver, liquid enamel; kiln fired
PHOTO BY RALPH GABRINER

Marjorie Simon
Yellow Circle Brooch | 2006

2.5 X 7.5 X 0.6 CM

Enamel, copper, sterling silver;
embossed, sifted, kiln fired, tab set

PHOTO BY RALPH GABRINER

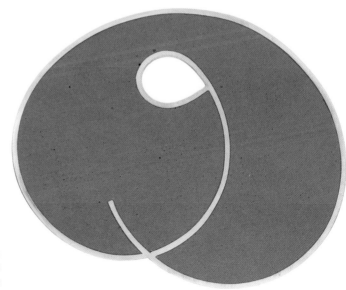

John Iversen

Red and Blue Enamel Pins | 1988–2007

RED, 8.9 X 7 X 0.2 CM
BLUE, 7.6 X 6.4 X 0.2 CM

Red: 18-karat gold; enamle an plein
Blue: gold-plated copper; enamle an plein

PHOTO BY ROBERT HENSLEIGH

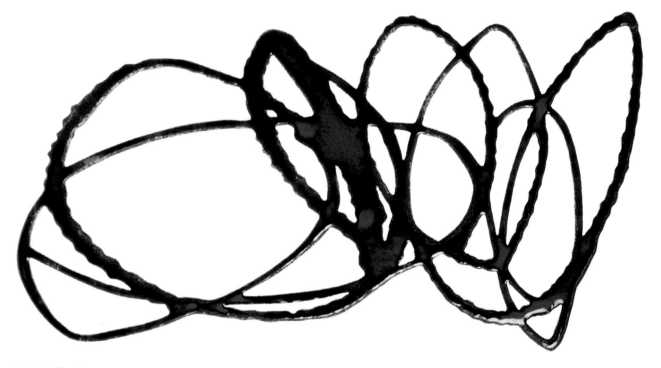

Michelle Donovan
Untitled | 2008
14.5 X 7.5 X 0.2 CM
Copper, enamel; sifted, kiln fired
PHOTO BY ARTIST

My work is an exploration of engineering and the processes through which I create complex objects that define space and form. By designing and cutting repetitive shapes for a skeleton of copper and fusing the form together with enamel, I explore the interdependence of the two materials. The enamel couldn't take shape without the metal as support, and the metal wouldn't remain an object without the introduction of the enamel. JIM NORTON

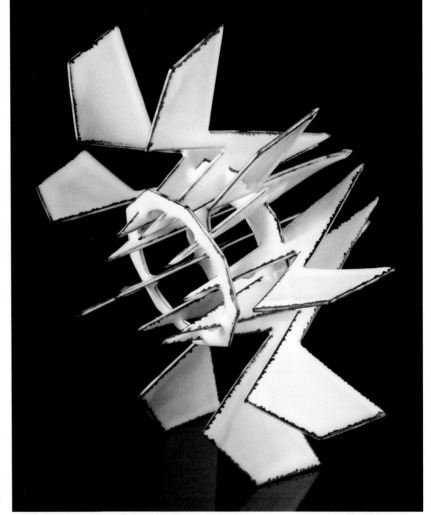

Jim Norton
Sputnik Structure | 2007
15 X 15 X 10 CM
Copper, enamel; dipped, kiln fired
PHOTO BY ARTIST

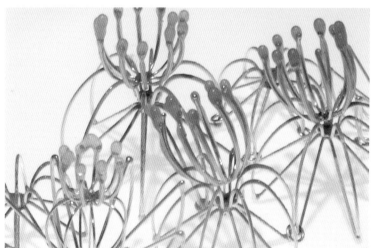

Kathy Voues

Lichen Necklace | 2007

DIAMETER, 31 CM

Sterling silver, enamel, silicone;
soldered, torch fired, micro welded

PHOTOS BY ARTIST

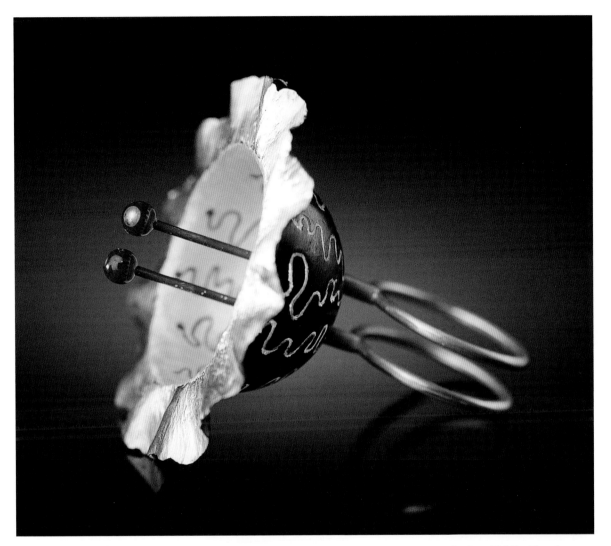

Anke AMO Akerboom

Nymphoides | 1989

4 X 4 X 4 CM

Sterling silver, enamel; fabricated, pressed,
hammered, plique-à-jour, émail en ronde bosse

PHOTO BY ARTIST

Annette Dam
*Everybody Has Got the Right
to a Cool Kitchen* | 2007
9 X 5.5 X 0.5 CM
Sterling silver, enamel; transfer
PHOTO BY ARTIST

Amelia Toelke
Untitled | 2006
5.1 X 7 X 0.3 CM
Enamel, copper, sterling silver; sifted
PHOTO BY ARTIST

Kate Bauman
Growths | 2007
30 X 25 X 1.3 CM
Copper, enamel, wallpaper;
sifted, kiln fired, melted
PHOTOS BY ARTIST

Leslie A. Schug
The Hostage | 2006
61 X 5.1 X 1.7 CM
Sterling silver, enamel, onyx, glass, key, enamel decal; sifted, kiln fired, bezel set
PHOTOS BY ARTIST

Michelle Parker
Sleep Tight | 2006
10.8 X 14 X 10.2 CM
Fine silver, sterling silver,
enamel; cloisonné, kiln fired
PHOTO BY SETH TICE-LEWIS PHOTOGRAPHY

Mer Almagro
Skull I | 2005

3 X 3.5 CM

Enamel, copper, onglaze colors, patina, sterling silver, freshwater pearls; painted, kiln fired, frame set

PHOTO BY ARTIST

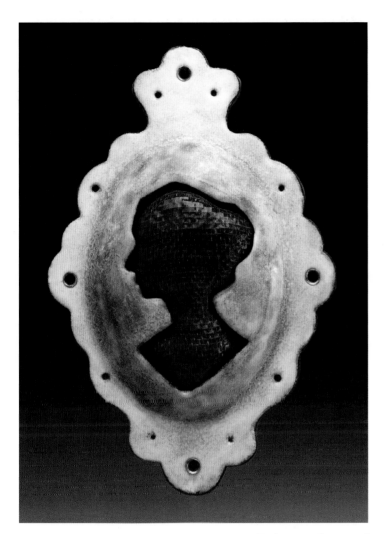

Rebecca Annand
Lady Brooch | 2006
16 X 10 X 6 CM
Copper, enamel, spring steel;
sifted, kiln fired, riveted
PHOTOS BY ARTIST

Joanna Gollberg
First All Me, Then Part Her | 2006
3.8 X 3.8 X 3.2 CM
Steel, enamel; wet packed, sifted, kiln fired
PHOTO BY ARTIST

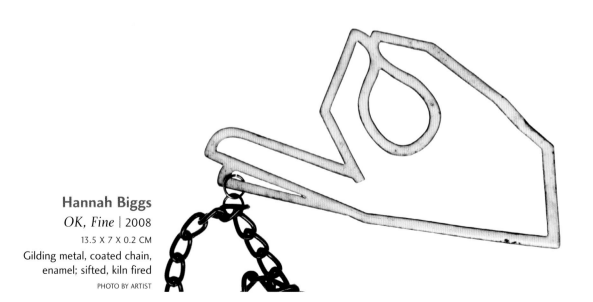

Hannah Biggs
OK, Fine | 2008
13.5 X 7 X 0.2 CM
Gilding metal, coated chain,
enamel; sifted, kiln fired
PHOTO BY ARTIST

Robert Ebendorf

The Lady with One Red Shoe | 2003

15.2 X 11.4 CM

Steel, enamel, enamel decals

PHOTO BY LINDA DARTY

Kate Bauman

Heirloom | 2006

6.9 X 6.9 X 0.6 CM

Copper, enamel; repoussé,
sifted, painted, kiln fired

PHOTO BY ARTIST

Sofia Björkman
Time | 2006
8 X 3 X 2 CM
Silver, enamel; cast
PHOTO BY ARTIST

Liz Schock
Autumn Leaves Necklace | 2007
27.9 X 25.4 X 3.8 CM
Copper, enamel, satin ribbon; kiln fired
PHOTO BY DEAN POWELL

Elizabeth Kaprow
Untitled Brooch | 2007
4.3 X 3.8 X 0.2 CM
Copper, sterling silver,
liquid enamel; kiln fired
PHOTO BY RALPH GABRINER

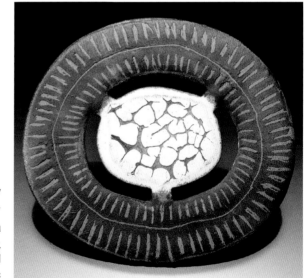

Abby Feldman
Neck Drop | 2005
CENTER, 8 X 5 X 0.7 CM
Copper, sterling silver,
enamel; sifted, kiln fired
PHOTO BY ARTIST

Eleanor Kennell
Untitled | 2008
6 X 3.6 X 1.1 CM
Sterling silver, enamel; sifted,
kiln fired, prong set
PHOTO BY KEN YANOVIAK

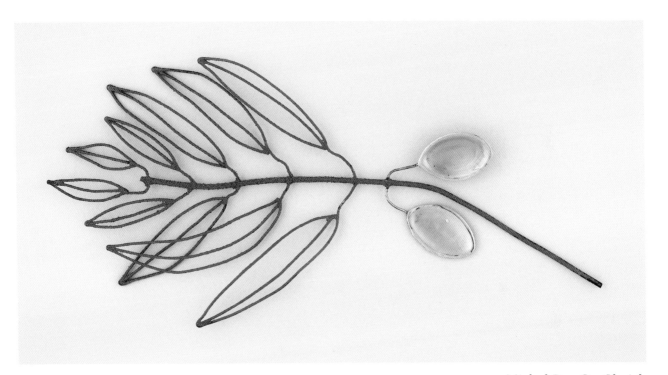

Michal Bar-On Shaish
Red Olive | 2008
14 X 6 X 1.5 CM
Iron binding wire, gold, enamel; sifted
PHOTO BY RAN PLOTNIZKY

Barbara Ryman

The Beauty of Innuendo IV | 2006

14 X 14 CM

Copper, enamel, silver; spun, etched, plated,
hand raised, pierced, under fired, joined

PHOTO BY JOHANNES KUHNEN

Angela Gerhard
Red Flower Brooch | 2008
7.6 X 8.9 X 1.3 CM
Copper, sterling silver, enamel;
sifted, etched, riveted, soldered
PHOTO BY ROBERT DIAMANTE

Jim Jordan

Peace Dove Christmas Ornament | 2007

15 X 10 X 1 CM

Sterling silver, gold, enamel, gold luster; repoussé

PHOTO BY JOE KORTH

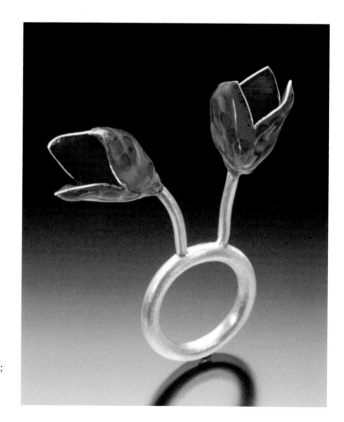

Sarah Hood

Firoza Ring | 1999

5 X 5 X 1.3 CM

Sterling silver, fine silver, enamel, glass beads; hand fabricated, soldered, sifted, kiln fired

PHOTO BY DOUG YAPLE

Lulu Lederman
The Blight Ring | 2006
4.5 X 3 X 3 CM
Copper, enamel; electroformed,
sifted, kiln fired, torch fired
PHOTO BY MARTY DOYLE

Mirek Gomolka
In Red | 2007
7 X 3 X 0.3 CM
Copper, steel, 22-karat gold,
enamel, bronze; kiln fired
PHOTO BY ARTIST

Danielle d'Usseau
Untitled | 2004
3 X 2 X 1.5 CM
Copper wire, enamel; woven, kiln fired
PHOTO BY AMY O'CONNEL

Dee Fontans

Eye Cups—Primaries Red | 1998

3.2 X 53.3 X 2.5 CM

Copper, enamel, 24-karat gold;
hydraulic pressed, sifted, kiln fired

PHOTO BY CHARLES LEWTON-BRAIN

Xiao Jia Ren
Untitled | 2008
VARIOUS DIMENSIONS
Fine silver, synthetic stones,
enamel; folded, domed, kiln fired
PHOTO BY JEREMY DILLON

Nina Ellis
Rings | 2003
EACH, 2.5 X 2 X 0.5 CM
Sterling silver, enamel; sifted
PHOTO BY ARTIST

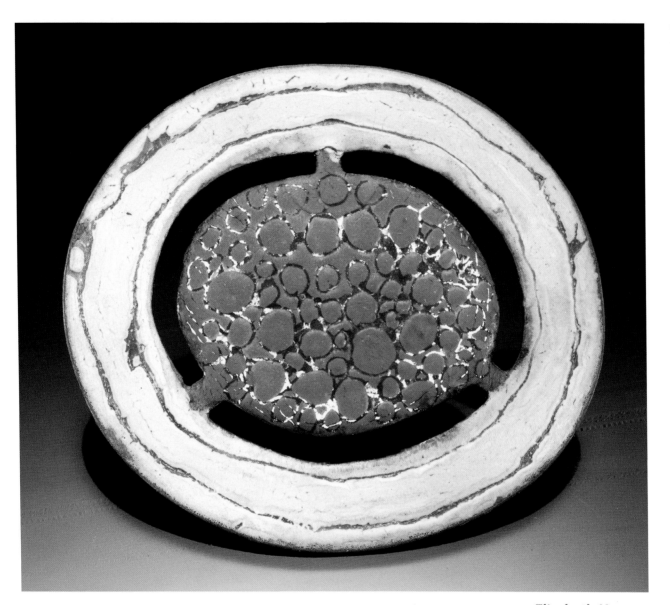

Elizabeth Kaprow
Untitled Brooch | 2007
5 X 4.4 X 0.2 CM
Copper, sterling silver, liquid enamel; kiln fired
PHOTO BY RALPH GABRINER

Rachel Gorman

Orange Blossom Brooch | 2007

6 X 8 X 1.5 CM

Copper, sterling silver, glass beads;
fused, sifted, kiln fired, saw pierced

PHOTO BY ARTIST

Kirsten Haydon
Ice Funnel, Ice Cups (Objects) | 2007
LARGEST, 8 X 6 X 4 CM
Copper, steel, enamel
PHOTO BY JEREMY DILLON

Elizabeth Turrell
Universal Declaration of Human Rights Series: Marker | 2007

75 X 50 X 1 CM

Industrial enamel, steel, enamel decal; drawn

PHOTOS BY ARTIST

My work is inspired by the memorials that commemorate war. 1999 was the 50th anniversary of the Universal Declaration of Human Rights, and I have added fragments of this text to my work. In the light of contemporary conflicts, I am compelled to make markers and memorials, both to remember individuals and to mark those conflicts. In today's world, these pieces could also be considered talismans. ELIZABETH TURRELL

Helen Carnac

Vitreous Enamel Vessels | 2008

LARGEST, 16 X 16 CM

Enamel, steel; wet processed,
sgraffito, kiln fired

PHOTOS BY ARTIST

Kye-Yeon Son
Innate Gesture 2007–6 (Brooch) | 2007
5.5 X 5.5 X 0.8 CM
Copper, enamel; soldered, sifted
PHOTO BY GEORGE GEORGAKAKOS

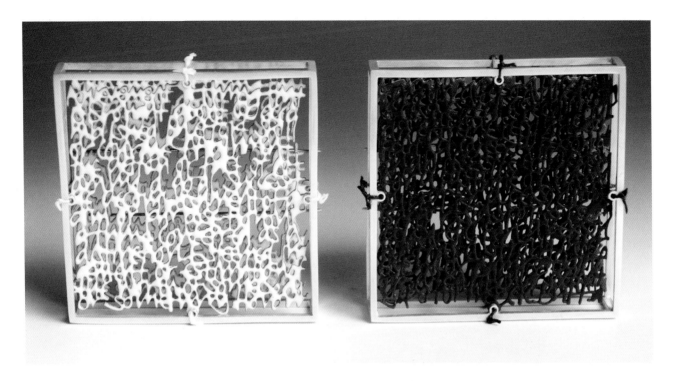

Jessica Turrell

Achievement Text Brooch and
Enthusiast Text Brooch | 2007

EACH, 6 X 6 X 1.2 CM

Sterling silver, copper, enamel,
linen thread; etched, sifted

PHOTOS BY ARTIST

Heechan Kim
The Origin of Love | 2007
17.7 X 12 CM
Copper, fine silver, enamel; wet packed, raised, kiln fired
PHOTO BY JACOB SNOWBARGER

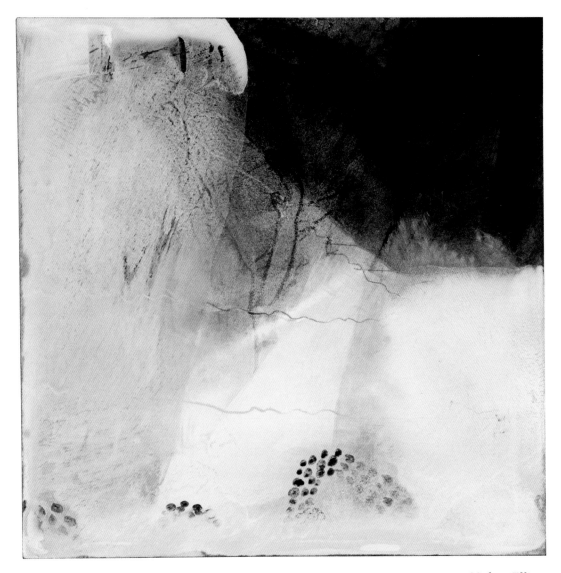

Helen Elliott
Silent Noise | 2007
30.5 X 30.5 X 3.8 CM
Porcelain enamel, jewelry enamel, steel,
wood; painted, sifted, mounted
PHOTO BY GREG STALEY

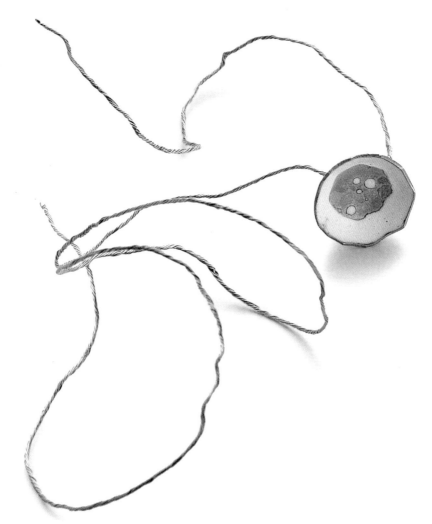

Patrizia Bonati

R2 (Earring) | 2003

1.8 X 5 X 2.2 CM

18-karat gold, enamel, gold
thread; chiseled, welded, twisted

PHOTO BY ARTIST

Giovanni Sicuro (Minto)

Doppio | 2006

2.2 X 5.9 CM

Silver, 24-karat gold, steel, enamel,
niello; hollow constructed

Michal Bar-On Shaish

Tire | 2008

DIAMETER, 2.5 CM

Copper, gold, enamel; plique-à-jour, sifted

PHOTO BY RAN PLOTNIZKY

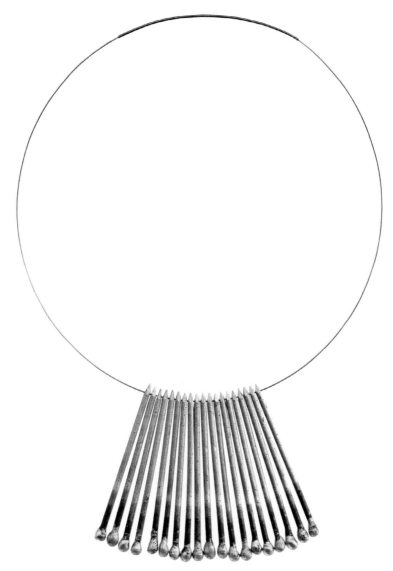

Niki Ulehla

19 Nails | 2008

21 X 15 X 0.3 CM

Galvanized steel nails, enamel,
22-karat gold, piano wire, sterling
silver; oxidized, torch fired

PHOTO BY ARTIST

Debbie Leh-Pargac

*Dancing Shaman Pre-Columbian
Ceremonial Neckpiece* | 2006

DIAMETER, 17 CM; EACH FIGURE, 2.5 X 2.5 CM

Copper, sterling silver, 24-karat gold,
enamel; die cut, under fired, etched

PHOTO BY JACK ZILKER

Olga Doutkevitch

The Card Ring | 2007

2.3 X 2.3 CM

Enamel, fine silver, 22-karat gold,
ruby, rose-cut diamonds; painted

GOLDSMITHING BY MICHAEL ELLIS
PHOTO BY MICHAEL ELLIS

Mary Heller

Ancient Rhythms | 2006

NECKLACE, 3 X 47 X 0.7 CM
PENDANT, 9 X 6 X 0.8 CM

22-karat gold, 20-karat gold, 24-karat
gold, enamel, fine silver, labradorite, jasper,
tourmaline; cloisonné, hand fabricated,
granulated, fused, bezel set

PHOTO BY CIRCLE CHANG PHOTOGRAPHY

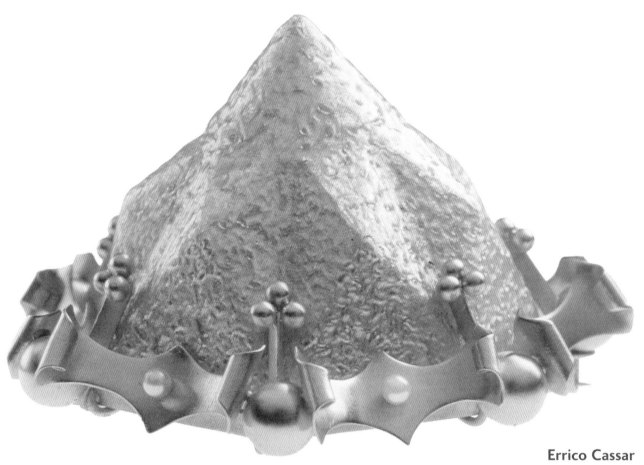

Errico Cassar
Untitled | 2001
3.1 X 5.5 CM
22-karat gold, pearls,
enamel, gold foil; sifted, kiln
fired, under fired, claw set
PHOTO BY ARTIST

Errico Cassar
Untitled | 2001
2.5 X 5.5 X 6.5 CM
22-karat gold, citrine, enamel, gold foil;
sifted, kiln fired, carborundum stone
ground, sanded, claw set
PHOTO BY ARTIST

Colette (AKA Colette Denton)
Oval Bracelet #3 | 1983
3.8 X 7 CM
Sterling silver, fine silver, 24-karat gold,
22-karat gold; cloisonné, painted, bezel set
PHOTOS BY ARTIST

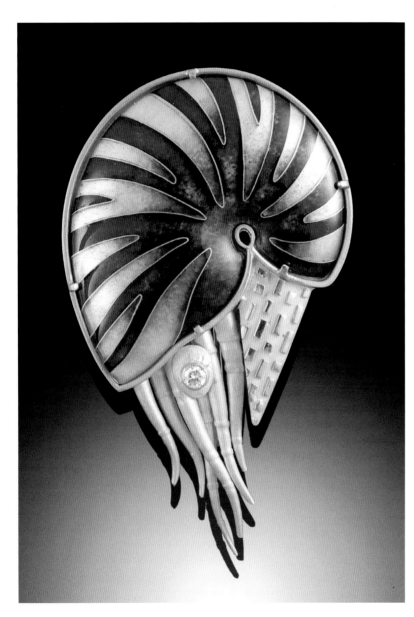

Amy Roper Lyons

Chambered Nautilus Pin #3 | 2007

5.6 X 3.8 X 0.8 CM

18-karat gold, 24-karat gold, enamel, diamond; prong set, cloisonné, fabricated, fused, formed, fold formed, hollow spicula

PHOTO BY ARTIST

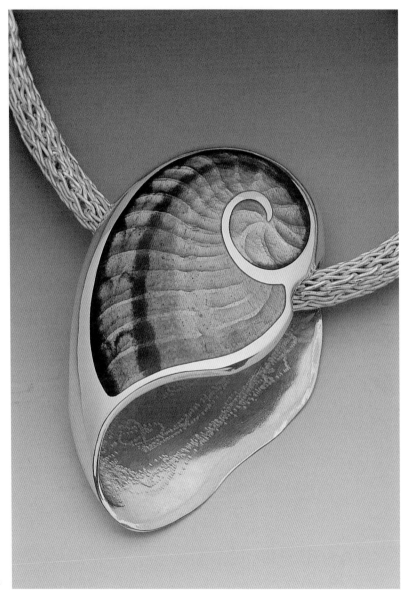

Kristin A. Anderson
Fantasy Shell Orange and Purple | 2003
7.5 X 5.5 X 2.5 CM
Sterling silver, enamel; wet packed, pierced,
carved, soldered, hammered, kiln fired
PHOTO BY STEVE MELTZER

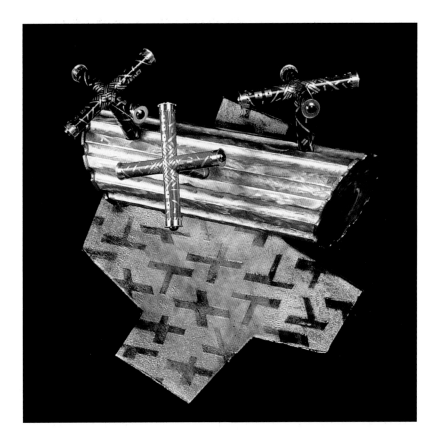

James Malenda
Station XI | 2006
61 X 61 X 46 CM

Copper, aluminum, fine silver,
sterling silver, 24-karat gold, enamel,
carnelians; sifted, stenciled

PHOTOS BY ARTIST

My work is unique because it combines very old, traditional handicraft techniques with the newest technological processes. Neither side predominates. HAGEN GAMISCH

Hagen Gamisch
Aedes Tellus | 2006
3 X 3 X 2 CM
Silver, enamel, tourmaline;
CAD, sand cast
PHOTO BY PETRA JASCHKE

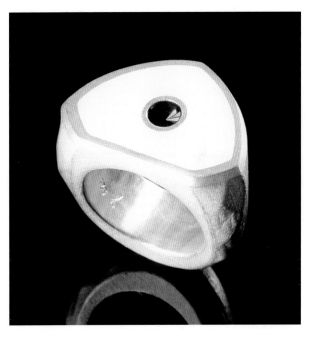

Jaime Frechette

Enameled Foil Maché Necklace | 2007

50.8 X 3.3 CM

Recycled copper wire, fine silver foil, enamel; hand formed, sifted, kiln fired, strung

PHOTO BY MEL MITTERMILLER

Lulu Lederman
Untitled | 2006
2.3 X 2.5 X 0.5 CM
Sterling silver, enamel; sifted, sugar fired
PHOTO BY MARTY DOYLE

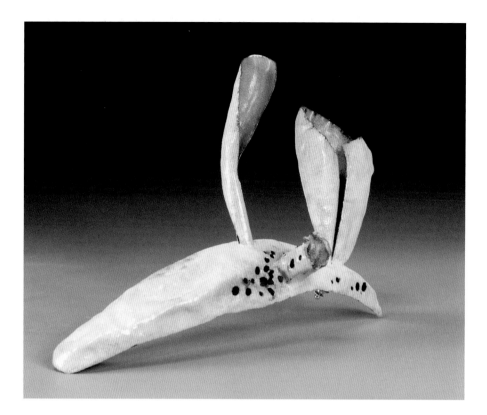

Emily Schuhmann
Exponential Growth I | 2008
12.7 X 7.6 X 27.9 CM
Copper, enamel; fused, shaped, sifted
PHOTOS BY ROBLY GLOVER

Emily Watson
The Graphic Body, Attachable No. 6 | 2003
16.5 X 5 X 3.8 CM
Copper, enamel, steel, magnets; electroformed,
fabricated, sifted, painted, kiln fired
PHOTO BY ARTIST

Leia Zumbro

Begin | 2007

8.5 X 3.5 X 3.5 CM

Copper, enamel; electroformed,
sifted, kiln fired, etched

PHOTO BY BLAKE LARUE

Yi Chen

Sea Creature #7 | 2008

6 X 12 X10 CM

Copper, enamel; torch fired, raised

PHOTOS BY ARTIST

Yoshiko Yamamoto
Object: Copper Mesh Form # 13 | 1998
14.6 X 7.6 X 7.6 CM
Copper, enamel; formed, sifted, kiln fired
PHOTOS BY DEAN POWELL

Liz Steiner

Rock Brooch | 2007

22 X 7 X 6 CM

Copper, enamel, string; electroformed,
sifted, kiln fired, knitted

PHOTO BY ARTIST

René Roberts

Tafoni Formation No. 2 | 2006

21 X 21 X 1.5 CM

Copper, enamel, glass stainers colors;
photoetched, wet packed, painted,
champlevé, wall mounted

PHOTO BY ARTIST

Kira Williams

Capture and Release | 2006

20 X 18 X 19 CM

Copper, enamel, polymer clay, acrylic
paint, patina, human hair; raised,
electroformed, stoned, painted

PHOTO BY HELEN SHIRK

Molly Groom Alter
Cancer 1–4 | 2006

22.9 X 365.8 X 17.8 CM

Copper, enamel, clear plastic sheeting,
stainless steel, mild steel; sifted

PHOTOS BY ARTIST

Abby Feldman

Swinging in Swampscott | 2006
CHAIR, 18 X 19 X 17 CM
Copper, sterling silver, string, enamel;
electroformed, sifted, kiln fired

PHOTO BY ARTIST

Fabrizio Tridenti
Tied Ring | 2007
6 X 3.5 X 2 CM
Silver, synthetic enamel;
soldered, fire enameled
PHOTO BY ARTIST

Transformations that occur through manipulated materials interest me. Snowflakes can begin from particles of dust, which grow unique crystalline structures. Similarly, a gemstone's flaw marks its growth. It's the flaw that makes the stone vivid and desirable. Somewhere in these flaws lives delirious and mysterious beauty. I look for beauty in the powerful instances that allude to the messiness of life. JESSICA KAHLE

Jessica Kahle
Crystalline Blush | 2007
7.5 X 9 X 2 CM
Mica, enamel, 18-karat gold; fabricated
PHOTO BY ARTIST

Sharon Massey
Ring | 2003
4 X 3 X 3 CM
Sterling silver, copper, enamel; sifted, fabricated
PHOTO BY ROBERT DIAMANTE

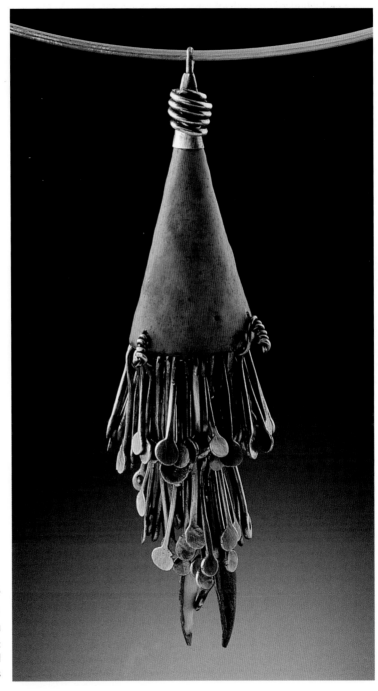

Steff Korsage
Yellow Cone Pendant | 2006
13.3 X 2.5 X 2.5 CM
Copper, sterling silver, enamel;
kiln fired, cold connected
PHOTO BY LARRY SANDERS

Jessica Calderwood
Sticky Fingers (Platter) | 2007
17.8 X 30.5 X 10.2 CM
Enamel, copper, brass; die formed,
water jet cut, electroformed, limoges
PHOTO BY ARTIST

Mirjam Hiller
Brooch | 2007
6 X 8 X 8 CM
Copper, sterling silver, steel,
enamel; brilliance fired
PHOTO BY PETRA JASCHKE

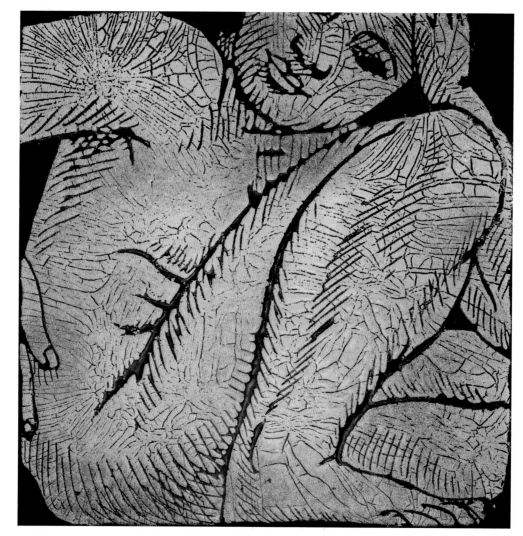

Jennifer Hodis
Vicki | 2008
15 X 15 X 0.3 CM
Copper, crackle enamel; kiln fired
PHOTO BY ART WORKS

This crackle piece was one of those 'one firing and it was complete' jobs. All the elements were lined up just right—the base color, the crackle color, the thickness, the lines in the drawing, and the light sifting on top. All the piece needed was the perfect time in the kiln. Pieces like this make enameling seem easy. Now, if I could just duplicate it! JENNIFER HODIS

Jutta Klingebiel
Ein Paar | 2002
EACH, 1.3 CM
18-karat gold, enamel; painted
PHOTO BY ARTIST

Sandra Ellen Bradshaw
On a Wing and a Prayer II | 2004
16.5 X 11.4 X 8.9 CM
Copper, brass, fine silver;
limoges, sifted, painted
PHOTO BY ARTIST

Nikki Couppee

Portrait (Brooch) | 2007

1.3 X 1.3 X 0.5 CM

Brass, copper, gold, sterling silver; cloisonné,
wet packed, prong set, bezel set

Madeline Noveck

Ring with Ancient Mesopotamian Nude Hero | 2007

2.1 X 2 X 1 CM

Sterling silver, enamel; cast, wet inlay

PHOTO BY D. JAMES DEE

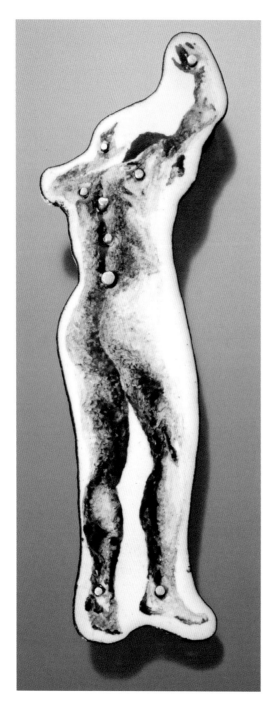

I am driven to portray man in a post-humanist world. I explore what it means to be a vulnerable individual, someone who is ambiguous in life, characterized only by his situation. My pieces are personal reminders that man is a small figure in the totality of existence. JOSEPH M. PILLARI

Joseph M. Pillari
Anonymity | 2007
8 X 2 X 0.5 CM
Copper, sterling silver, enamel; sifted, kiln fired, limoges, riveted
PHOTO BY KEN YANOVIAK

Joyaux Marisol

La Belle Révérence | 2007

8 X 8 CM

Copper, enamel; chased, repoussé

PHOTO BY ARTIST

Kristi Rae Wilson

Hymnal Brooch | 2007

3 X 5 X 6 CM

Copper, found objects, enamel, stainless steel;
over fired, tab constructed, electroformed

PHOTO BY ARTIST

Inspired by traditional adornment, I create wearable art influenced by cultures that are consumed with faith. My interest in theology is really an obsession. Everything I construct is sketched around the recreation, modernization, and reflection of belief-based embellishment. TARYN LINDSAY BACKUS

Taryn Lindsay Backus
Spoonfuls of Virtues | 2008

CREDENCE, 24 X 9 X 3 CM
MORALITY, 22 X 8 X 5 CM
DEVOTION, 23 X 7 X 4 CM

Copper, bronze, felt, thread, enamel; sifted, kiln fired

PHOTO BY KEN YANOVIAK

Katharine Redford
Blue Buckle | 2007
5.1 X 8.9 X 1.3 CM
Copper, enamel; etched
PHOTO BY ARTIST

Lih-Chuan Lin
The Glacé Icing Fruits | 2006
9.5 X 7.5 X 3 CM
Sterling silver, copper, enamel,
horsehair; chased, repoussé, sifted
PHOTO BY KUN-LUNG TSAI

Kristin Mitsu Shiga

Evolve | 2005

19 X 5 X 7 CM

Copper, sterling silver, enamel, pearls; electroformed, fabricated, sifted, wet packed, ground, sandblasted

PHOTOS BY DAN KVITKA

Sophie Hughes
Artichoke | 2007
10 X 10 CM
Copper, enamel, thistle blossom;
pierced, riveted, sifted, kiln fired
PHOTO BY PETER HARRIS

Wendy Yothers

A Pull Toy for a Czaravich | 1998

10 X 12 X 5 CM

Sterling silver, enamel, diamonds, hematite, rubber O rings; fabricated, cloisonné, raised, spun

PHOTO BY DICK DUANE

All of my work seems to hark back to history and make a contemporary comment on it. This piece is a low-tech automaton with classical double-hulled construction for the enamel vessel, and precious gems hiding screws and bolts. Inside the egg is a fabricated silver chicken foot that can be unscrewed and installed on the round end of the outside of the egg, making it freestanding. WENDY YOTHERS

Helen Aitken-Kuhnen
Mushroom Boxes | 1980
6 X 5 X 5 CM
Sterling silver, enamel; raised, engraved
PHOTO BY JOHANNES KUHNEN

Gail MacMillan-Leavitt
Sea Squirt Necklace-Sculpture | 2008
17 X 28 X 4.5 CM
Copper, lucite, nylon, resin, enamel;
limoges, cold connected
PHOTO BY ARTIST

Cynthia Lewis

Global Warming | 2008

22.9 X 25.4 X 9.5 CM

Copper, enamel, sterling silver,
unique bronze, glass; sifted

PHOTO BY ARTIST

Susanne Miller
Broche | 2005
LARGEST, 10 X 3 CM
Silver, copper, enamel
PHOTOS BY ARTIST

Barbara Smith

Self-Portrait with My Brother (Butterfly Brooch) | 2008

6.4 X 6.4 X 1.3 CM

Copper, sterling silver, stainless steel, hair; die formed, chased, fabricated, sifted, painted, etched, oxidized

Ruth Zelanski
Synaptic Pendant (I) | 2006
9 X 8.5 X 1 CM
Copper, enamel, sterling silver,
wool, glass, silk; electroformed,
sifted, needle felted
PHOTO BY ARTIST

This piece represents a fight—a fight for unprecious materials! I believe that a valuable piece of jewelry doesn't have to contain gold and diamonds. The value lies in the time and love you give to the material.

LISA BJÖRKE

Lisa Björke
Just As Right | 2007
8 X 11 X 4 CM
Yarn, copper, enamel, rose quartz, wallpaper, epoxy glue; crocheted, oven heated
PHOTO BY ARTIST

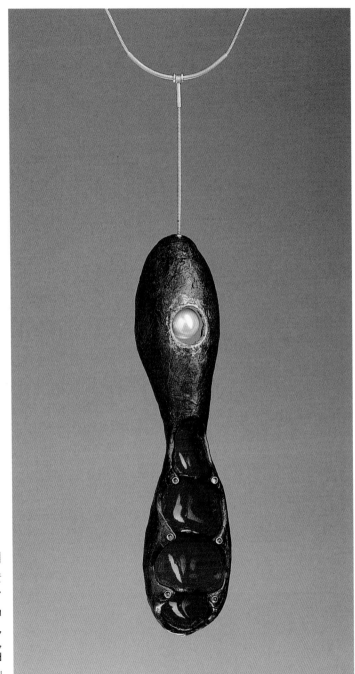

> This piece symbolizes the
> journeys that take place in
> Thomas Mann's novel—the
> journey through arched canals,
> through unrequited desire, envy,
> and passion. VALERIE MITCHELL

Valerie Mitchell
*Death in Venice Pendant
for the Opera* | 1997
18 X 4 CM
Copper, enamel, peridot, pearl,
gold leaf, silver; oxidized,
electroformed, kiln fired
PHOTO BY PIA TORELLI

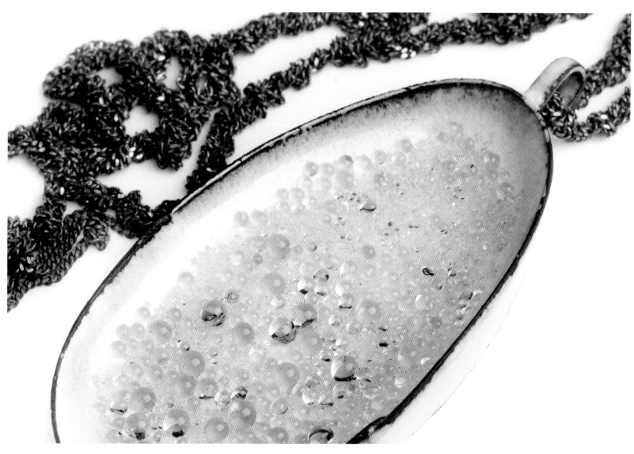

Claudia Milić
Untitled | 2008
8 X 4 X 1 CM
Tombak, enamel, glass pearls; sifted
PHOTO BY TOM NASSAL

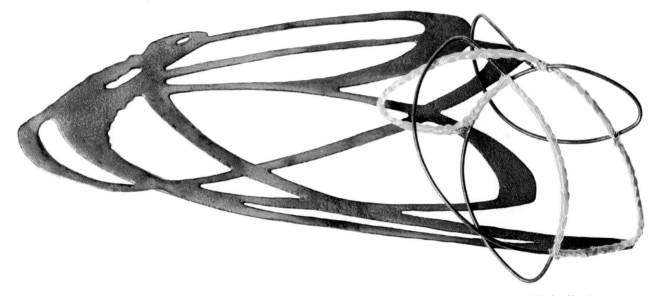

PHOTO BY ARTIST

Michelle Donovan
Untitled | 2008
18 X 7 X 3 CM
Copper, stainless steel, fine silver;
crocheted, sifted, wet packed, kiln fired

Renée Menard
Desert Rose | 2006

17.8 X 17.8 X 10.2 CM

Copper, enamel; formed,
fabricated, kiln fired

PHOTO BY HELEN SHIRK

I am fascinated and inspired by nature—by its shapes, colors, and forms. Changing patterns of light and shadow from dawn to dusk are part of the fascination. The color, reflection, and transparency of enameled pieces are expressive elements that mirror but don't mimic the natural world. RENÉE MENARD

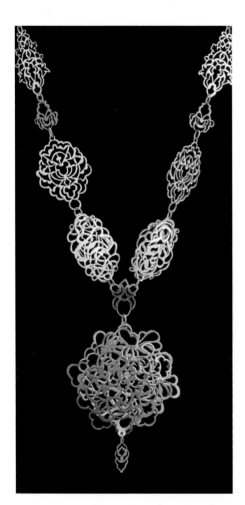

Taryn Lindsay Backus
Personal Rituals | 2007
54 X 22 X 3 CM
Copper, sterling silver, enamel; sifted, kiln fired
PHOTOS BY KEN YANOVIAK

Beth M. Biggs

Seduced Series: Lily | 2007

1.5 X 13 X 20 CM

Sterling silver, copper, enamel; cast, chased, repoussé, hand fabricated

PHOTO BY DREW GILBERT

In this body of work I'm making a direct link between the seduction of flowers and feminine desire. Each pendant hangs from a chain of leaves, while the clasps depict snake heads. The presence of the snake suggests the Garden of Eden and symbolizes the relationship of nature, the feminine, desire, and, ultimately, blame. BETH M. BIGGS

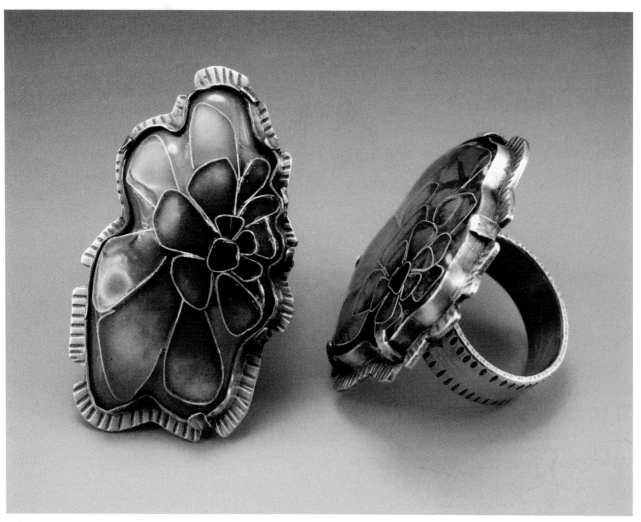

Amanda Outcalt
Floral Cloisonné Ring Pair | 2006
EACH, 4 X 3 X 3 CM
Sterling silver, enamel; cloisonné
soldered, wet packed, bezel set
PHOTO BY ARTIST

Emi Ando

Umbrella (Nukumori) Necklace | 2007

16.5 X 16 X 0.6 CM

Sterling silver, copper, enamel; sifted, kiln fired

PHOTO BY ADRIAN ORDENANA

Lisa Björke
Morbid Creature | 2007
10 X 7 X 7 CM
Yarn, epoxy glue, enamel, copper, silver,
amethyst; crocheted, oven heated, oxidized
PHOTO BY ARTIST

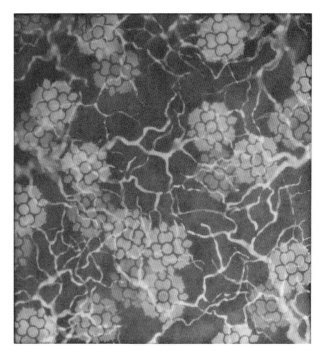 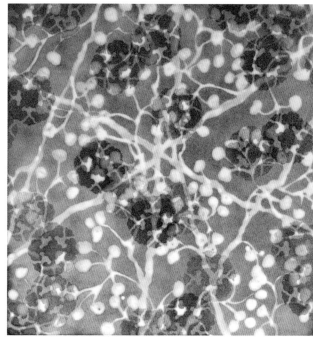

Gretchen Goss

Gesture + Ornament: Fagus sylvatica/Pyrus alnifolia | 2006

41 X 88 X 1 CM

Enamel, copper; sifted, painted

PHOTO BY ARTIST

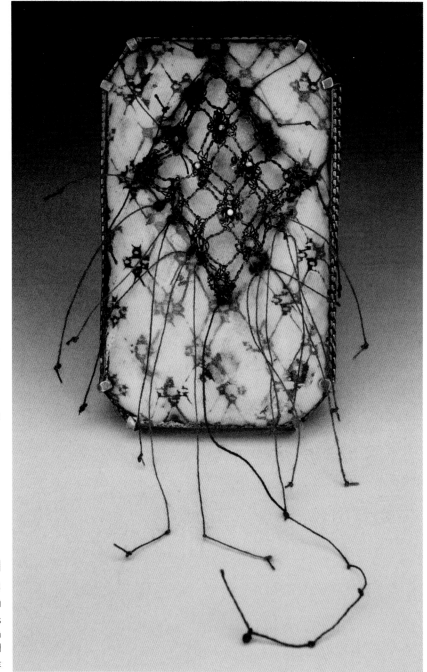

In my most recent body of work, I am purposely creating formal and personal dichotomies, elaborating on the nuances, imperfections, and human associations that can exist in something hand-labored. I do this by weaving voluminous frays or manipulated fragile layers that seem to be pulling away from their stable exteriors of highly decorative enameled patterns in metal.

ALICIA JANE BOSWELL

Alicia Jane Boswell
Salient | 2008

6.3 X 4.5 X 2.5 CM

Copper, sterling silver, stainless steel, thread, enamel; bobbin laced, etched, champlevé, sifted

PHOTO BY JILL GREENE

Lydia V. Gerbig-Fast

Nitric Blue Neckpiece | 2007

4 X 21 X 22 CM

14-karat gold, 18-karat gold bi-metal, sterling
silver, enamel, copper, opals, pink imperial topaz;
sifted, kiln fired, cold connected

PHOTO BY ARTIST

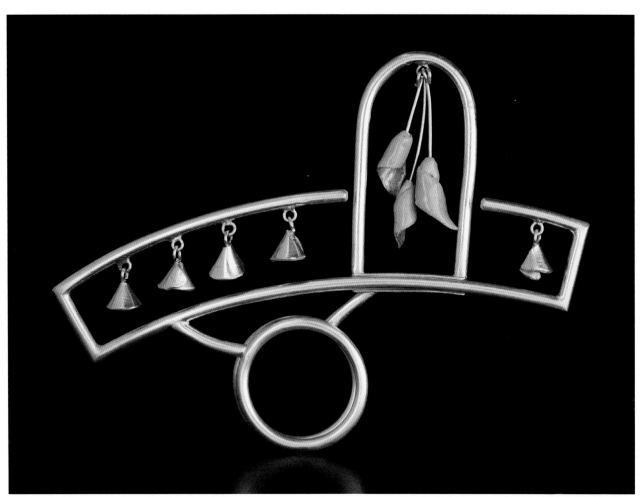

Tura Sugden
Pollination Rings | 2007
7 X 8 X 0.3 CM
Sterling silver, fine silver,
enamel; sifted, kiln fired
PHOTO BY ADRIAN ORDEÑANA

Francis Willemstijn
Madder | 2006
6 X 12 X 2 CM
Silver, enamel, wood, garnets, madder
PHOTO BY ARTIST

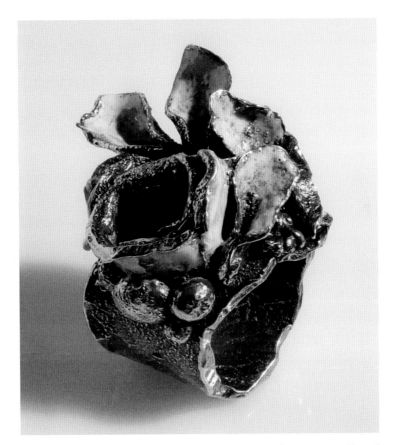

Jenny Edlund
Amor Fati Series: Ring | 2004
4.5 X 3 X 2 CM
Sterling silver, enamel; gilded, oxidized
PHOTO BY ARTIST

Susan McMurray

Grass Vessel | 2007

10.5 X 8 X 8 CM

Sterling silver, dirt,
enamel; fabricated

PHOTO BY ARTIST

Kye-Yeon Son
Innate Gesture 2007–10 (Brooch) | 2007
8.5 X 6 X 3 CM
Copper, enamel; soldered, electroformed, sifted
PHOTO BY GEORGE GEORGAKAKOS

Contributing Artists

Acknowledgments

I am incredibly grateful for the expertise, enthusiasm, and generosity of juror Sarah Perkins. Her wisdom, reflection, and diligence made the challenging process of jurying thousands of images a complete pleasure and a valuable learning experience. Sarah's keen sensibilities have shaped a truly unique collection of work.

I deeply appreciate the continued support of all the jewelers and metalsmiths around the world who send images to be considered for this series. At their heart, these books are a celebration of their talent, creative vision, and dedication to their medium. I also wish to thank the galleries, schools, and organizations that promote contemporary metalwork, teach and inspire others, and advocate our publications.

Publishing is an amazing collaborative adventure. It takes a talented team of professionals to manage the multitude of details that comprise these books. Paige Gilchrist, Kathy Sheldon, Julie Hale, Dawn Dillingham, and Beth Sweet provided indispensable editorial support. Chris Bryant and Shannon Yokeley supplied first-rate assistance in the art department, and Matt Shay gave us a truly gorgeous layout and design. Todd Kaderabek and Lance Wille kept us on schedule, and Terry Taylor's trusted second opinion was, as always, offered with speed and grace. I value your talent, effort, and friendship every day.

—**Marthe Le Van**

About the Juror

Sarah Perkins received her MFA from Southern Illinois University–Carbondale in 1992 and is currently a professor of art and head of the Metals Area at Southwest Missouri State University–Springfield. Perkins has shown her work both nationally and internationally. She has participated in invitational and competitive group exhibitions and in one-person shows, including the Color and Light: International Enamel Exhibition in India; the Masterworks Invitational Exhibition in Ontario, Canada, which was sponsored by the Enamelist Society; the traveling exhibition The Art of Gold, which was sponsored by the Society of North American Goldsmiths; and Everyday Ceremonies: Work of Sarah Perkins at the Arkansas Decorative Arts Museum in Little Rock, Arkansas.

Perkins' work has appeared in *Metalsmith, Ornament, American Craft*, and in many books on enameling and metalsmithing. Her work is also included in the permanent collections of the Brooklyn Museum in Brooklyn, New York, the Ornamental Metal Museum in Memphis, Tennessee, and the Long Beach Museum of Art in Long Beach, California.

Perkins has taught workshops at the Penland School of Crafts in Penland, North Carolina; the Arrowmont School of Arts and Crafts in Gatlinburg, Tennessee; the California College of Arts in Oakland, California; Tainan National University of the Arts in Taiwan; and the University of the West of England in Bristol.